D1002727

178
COMMUNICATION
Facts, Tips, and Ideas

A Communispond Guide To Making The Workplace Work

COMMUNISPOND™

Routledge
Taylor & Francis Group

NEW YORK AND LONDON

First published 2006 by Routledge
270 Madison Ave, New York, NY 10016

Routledge is an imprint of the Taylor & Francis Group

ISBN 978-0-976-1569-1-8

Contents

Prologue:

"What We've Got Here Is a Failure to Communicate"

It's not often an organization problem is enshrined by a line in a movie, but it happened in 1967. In the 1967 film, *Cool Hand Luke*, its eponymous character memorialized the single most difficult problem of management and the workplace: "What we've got here is a failure to communicate."

The line was named one of top 100 movie quotations by the American Film Institute, putting it on a par with "Frankly, my dear, I don't give a damn" and "Go ahead, make my day."

Today, when you hear it spoken, it is usually in a humorous or ironic context and played for laughs. But it's worth remembering that in the climactic moment of the film, right after Luke delivers the line (it was the second time the line had been spoken), he is shot to death. The scene is a symbolic statement of the seriousness of communication problems.

Communication is indeed a serious business. Every organization has memories of communication failure, and it seems every disaster we read about in the newspapers includes some form of it, either as a cause or an aggravator. No thoughtful manager will deny the importance of clear communication—or the joys of working in a place where people truly understand each other.

At Communispond, we see the importance of communication every day. Our work as trainers and consultants brings us into close contact with people suffering the consequences of poor communication. And it has allowed us to witness many communication triumphs.

It has also given us a substantial stock of facts, tips, and ideas about communication, which we regularly share in our weekly email newsletter, *The Echo*, edited tirelessly and intelligently by our National Director of Faculty, Wayne Turmel.

This book represents our attempt to collect some of Communispond's communication wisdom in one place. Like much of human wisdom, it comes in small bits. We've tried to organize the bits by consolidating them into recognizable categories. We hope that makes them useful, but we have also tried to keep them brief and engaging enough that we suspect most people will simply read them in the order they appear.

Some of the bits will likely surprise you. Some will confirm things you already know. Some will make you laugh. And if you laugh, that's fine. Communication is indeed a serious business, but it doesn't have to be humorless.

"Great Moments in Communication"

1,000,000 YEARS AGO, EARLY HUMANS DISCOVER STAGE FRIGHT

Public Speaking

Glossophobia

Everyone knows about stage fright and the fear of public speaking. Do you know the proper term for this fear?

The psychological term for stage fright is "glossophobia," from the Greek word gloss, meaning tongue, and phobia, meaning fear.

A wise man once said that when you can name something, you begin to conquer your fear of it. Now you know what to call those feelings you can control with practice.

Five Myths About Stage Fright

Author Ivy Naistadt describes five popular myths that make our natural nervousness about speaking in public worse than it has to be. According to her book, *Speak Without Fear*, there are five misconceptions about stage fright:

1. *Nervousness = Weakness.* Don't believe it for a minute. Everyone is nervous.

2. *My nervousness is worse than everyone else's.* What, you know everyone else?

3. *I have to be perfect.* Well, a worthy aspiration, but you'd be the first ever.

4. *I have to be a comedian.* No, your message has to be interesting and relevant. Not the same thing at all.

5. *It's all over if I make a mistake.* No it's not. And unless you make it obvious, there's a good chance your audience may not know or care that you messed up.

Remember these five myths next time you start panicking about a presentation.

Communicating Passion

Increasingly, senior leaders in organizations want to know how to deliver company news in a way that ignites passion and motivates the audience. Remember to ask yourself, "So what?"

The most common mistake presenters make is to think that the more important the message, the more important the supporting data becomes. As a result, presentations become front-loaded with numbers and charts. Here's where that question comes in:

What does all this mean *to your audience*? "Numbers are up" is good news. So what? If numbers are bad, what does it mean to your audience? What action items are expected once they have the information? Give them only what they need to know to support that action item or recommendation. If they want more, they'll ask for it—that's what Q and A is for.

Give your audience a reason to care about your subject, then give it to them in a way that shows what it means to them. Appeal to their emotions, and let your own passion shine through.

We often say that true leaders communicate with passion and enthusiasm, but what does that mean? Here's what an audience perceives as passion:

What they see
- Open, expansive gestures
- Energized body language
- Solid eye contact, as if you're trying to reach each person individually

What they hear
- Strong volume
- Lots of inflection
- Use of positive, colorful language

Concentrating on data or the content of your message can drain concentration from your delivery of the message. Practice, practice, practice so that the content and media are second nature; then work on what they see and hear to create the same passion in your audience that you feel.

Dress Like a Winner

A recent study in the journal *Psychology of Sports and Exercise* found that if you want to gain a measurable edge over your opponent, stand up straight and dress like a pro. Sound familiar?

The study showed that when athletes were shown a video of prospective opponents, they were much less confident of victory if the subject displayed good posture, a genial demeanor, and dressed in a clean uniform. Conversely, if the subject slouched, frowned and didn't wear a sharp-looking uniform, opponents went into competition more likely to believe they would win.

The same goes for presentations. When you're trying to persuade an audience, do you look like a winner?

Distractions

Far be it from us to tell you how to dress for your audience, but a solid professional look is crucial to getting your point across, without distracting your audience. Here is a list of five common wardrobe mistakes business presenters make:

- *Too much jewelry.* Clanking bracelets and flashing, dangling earrings can be a distraction to the audience.

- *Short ties.* A tie should hang to the top of the belt buckle.

- *Skirts that are too short* (a distraction on female presenters, a total showstopper on men) are not only often inappropriate for business, but restrict motion and force presenters to stand still with their feet too close together.

- *Tight suit jackets.* Anything that restricts your ability to gesture comfortably is counter-productive. Try leaving the jacket unbuttoned.

- *Anything with Mickey Mouse* (or other cartoon characters) on it, unless you're presenting at Disney. Cute wardrobe touches frequently undermine credibility.

Don't Write it Out Completely

"Never write down your speeches beforehand; if you do, you may perhaps be a good declaimer, but will never be a debater."

Lord Chesterfield's advice to his son is true. By writing everything out word-for- word, you become attached to the words exactly as they are; there is no room for moving away from the text. You become a declaimer (a reader of what's there) rather than someone who can use the key points to answer questions, rephrase things the audience doesn't understand, and sound as if you're creating it spontaneously.

Make good notes by all means, but don't get tied to a script if you want to be able to think on your feet.

The Art of the Abstract

Ever heard of an abstract?

In academic circles, an abstract is a shortened version of a paper, much like an executive summary. When referring to oral presentations, an abstract is a single visual that contains the point, whether it's a call to action, a warning, or a vital piece of information.

When preparing a presentation, think about your abstract. If you had to put the main idea or recommendation on one slide, what would it be?

One last thing: *do it*. You'll save time, energy, and your audience's patience.

The Trouble With Troubleshooting

Presenters frequently lose face with their audiences by looking inept while struggling with the technology.

Think about the problems you've encountered when presenting. Computers crash, projectors don't project, the file won't open… What has been worse, the problem or the missteps and wasted time associated with overcoming it?

When something happens with the technology, there are only so many things you can do, most of which should have been done prior to beginning your presentation:
- Check your connections
- Reboot the computer
- Try another computer

If none of that works, then go to plan B. You do have a plan B, right?

- Have one clean copy of your presentation for emergency photocopying and handouts.

- Have your presentation on a disk as well as the hard drive of your computer.

- Practice your presentation so you're not completely reliant on your PowerPoint presentation for your notes.

Don't go crazy and waste the audience's time. Smile, breathe deeply and give them what you have anyway, confident that your message is solid.

Avoiding Dry Mouth

Ever seen a speaker cough incessantly, clear her throat constantly, or go dry in the middle of a sentence? Worse, have you ever been that speaker? Here are some tips for keeping your mouth and throat comfortable during presentations:

- Do have cool water on hand in an attractive glass. You don't want to mess with pouring water during your presentation, and ice in the water can cause spills or clink together, displaying your nervousness or even causing you to choke if you drink carelessly.

- Ice water can also cause tightening of the vocal cords, which can lead to other problems including a sore throat afterwards.

- Make sure you have a secure, flat surface on which to place your water. You don't need to add spilling to the list of possible distractions to your presentation.

- Don't drink coffee or other caffeinated beverages during your presentation. What, you're not nervous enough?
- Finish throat lozenges or hard candy before you begin to talk.

- Take a nice, slow, deep breath in through your mouth before you speak to make sure there's nothing in your airway or mouth that will cause you to cough.

Remember, it's the little things the audience sees that affect their perception of you as a presenter. Don't let unimportant details trip you up.

Coffee Is for Your Audience

Many presenters use caffeinated drinks to help them charge up for a presentation. They may find they do more harm than good.

Studies of the physical condition of people in various stressful situations, including giving short presentations, show that the average person creates large amounts of adrenaline and cortisol, often known as the "stress hormone."

In fact, they produce the same amount of stimulation as seven cups of coffee, which helps explain some of the symptoms of stage fright such as shaky hands, lack of concentration, and nervous bladder.

Be careful not to overdo the stimulants before a presentation. Your body is taking care of that for you.

Volume, Volume, Volume

As more and more communication is technologically driven and assisted, it's easy to neglect a factor of good communication that is as old as speech itself—volume.

When we face a room full of live people, it's easy to see the faces at the back of the room and adjust your volume accordingly. When you use a microphone, it's much easier to depend on the technology to make sure our voices can be heard effectively.

The color and inflection in our speech is largely the physical result of stretching the muscles and increasing the amount of air that we expel. These are directly connected to volume as well. It is always easier for technology to adjust to high volume and turn the gain down, than it is to turn it up and project flat, colorless language at a higher volume.

Speak to the audience, not the microphone.

Use Handouts for Audience Control

Handouts can frequently be a distraction to audiences and presenters alike. Control how your audience gets and uses them and they can help you maintain focus and get buy-in.

Don't hand out information packets or handouts until you absolutely have to. When you do, explain to them what's in the handout; e.g., "These are just the slides I've prepared." Then politely direct your audience not to flip ahead but to stay with you.

During your presentation, when you have to flip past a page, let the audience know what page you want them to go to and what they're missing. That way they don't suspect you're trying to hide something. They will be less tempted to read everything if you acknowledge the content and ask for their cooperation. They can then go back and read it at their leisure.

If a page has a lot of text or data, direct them to the exact place on the document you want them to read: "In the second paragraph, first bullet..." The audience will usually comply.

Be directive and remove any curiosity and the audience will be less distracted by the handout and more focused on your message.

Walking or Standing Still?

Is it better to stand still or move around during a presentation?

Both have their purposes. Standing in one place makes you look confident and credible and makes it easy to make eye contact with your audience. Moving around allows you to attract their attention, get closer to them and appear more energetic and interesting.

The trick is to understand when each is appropriate. When speaking or making an important point, plant yourself, make eye contact, and deliver. If you're going to move, move on transitions when you're not speaking, find a new location, plant yourself, and find another set of eyes.

Walking while talking distracts from your message and reduces your ability to exercise good "Eye-Brain Control®." Walk, then talk. You'll be amazed at the difference it makes.

How Much Time?

Many presenters, especially subject-matter experts, confuse the time allotted for a presentation with how long the presentation should be.

The length of a presentation should be based on more than simply how much time you have. Here are some determining factors:

- How long is the audience's attention span? As a rule, it's shorter than you think.

- What is their stated interest in the subject? If they have a high degree of interest going in, you've bought yourself more time.

- How strong are the benefits to them? If there isn't a powerful incentive to them to stay engaged, shorter is better.

Plan a short presentation and a healthy question and answer session. That way, the audience will determine the length of the presentation and the level of detail they need. If you've done your job well, they may give you more time than they allotted—and it will be *their* idea.

Use of Lecterns Diminishing

Fewer presenters at corporate functions are using a lectern. An informal survey of hotel catering managers reports they are providing fewer lecterns to meeting rooms. Particularly in the case of large events, new projection, lighting, and microphone technology means presenters are expected to be "front and center."

This is actually a good thing. Audience studies show presenters who work without a lectern are perceived as more confident and professional. Presenters who work without a lectern:

- Stand erect and without barriers to their audience

- Can move and gesture more effectively

- Add life to the presentation: movement and color attract the audience's attention and increase their retention of points made

Using a Microphone

"Amplification is the vice of modern oratory."
- Thomas Jefferson (1782)

You'd think today's small, wireless microphones would make "amplification" an asset and not a problem, yet many people don't use this wonderful technology as well as they might. Here are some *do's* and *don'ts*...

Do keep your own volume up—many presenters think because they have a microphone they can speak less energetically. This can lead to monotone delivery and non-words—and the audience will be less engaged.

Don't rely on the microphone. The higher a microphone is set, the higher the chances for feedback and static. Better to have the microphone set a little low and compensate with your voice.

Don't hook a Lavalier mic to moving clothing. Any place clothes rub or move (like the lapel of an open jacket) is a good chance for unwanted and annoying noise. Put it somewhere close to the center of your body that will stay put. Near the top of a secure necktie is a good bet.

Do get there early and test the technology. Will it work? Is it set too loud (always better to have to turn it down than have to crank it up)? Where are the "hot spots" where feedback will interfere with your presentation?

Your comfort with the technology is a major component in the audience's perception of your professionalism and effectiveness.

Practice Overcomes Obstacles

Winston Churchill had a slightly cleft palate and a stammer and was told he'd never speak normally, let alone in public.

James Earl Jones, who has one of the most recognizable and most highly compensated voices in the English-speaking world, stammered so badly he was rendered mute as a child.

The Greek orator Demosthenes had a stammer that made him painfully shy and many considered him stupid, until he became known as the wisest man in Athens.

What each of the examples has in common, besides the obstacles, is the desire to overcome a problem and a willingness to practice relentlessly. Rather than surrender and simply vanish into the crowd, these speakers took every opportunity to develop their talent. Whether through professional help, like Jones had, or self-discipline like Churchill, each was able to overcome major obstacles to their success and became renowned for their speaking ability.

Speaking well is largely a combination of motor skills. It gets better with practice. The more opportunities you give yourself to speak in public, the better you will become. Never refuse an opportunity to kick off a meeting, introduce a speaker, or make your point at a seminar.

Project Energy with Gestures

It makes sense that gestures make our communication more memorable and engaging. What makes a "good" gesture?

- Gestures should go "inside-out." By moving your gestures away from your body, rather than toward it, you make your gestures appear bigger and more purposeful.

- Gestures should be above the waist. Your audience wants to see what you're doing.

- Use a whole hand, rather than a single finger, to point. Open hands appear less aggressive than an accusing finger.

- Gestures don't have to convey exactly the subject you're talking about. This is conversation, not interpretive dance.

Gestures and Math

A recent study by the University of Chicago shows that children (and probably your audiences) learn when gestures and speech are both used in teaching.

In the study, "Children Learn when Their Teacher's Gestures and Speech Differ," (Singer and Goldin-Meadow), 160 third- and fourth-graders were taught math skills in different ways. One group of teachers used gestures to help explain concepts like grouping numbers, and one group did not. The group that used gestures got better results.

This may seem obvious, but it makes an important point: the gestures used were not simply the normal gestures used when speaking. They were *conscious, descriptive gestures* that sometimes contained different (but not contradictory) information than what the teacher was saying orally.

Careful attention to the gestures used gave the students both oral and visual cues, increasing the amount of information stored and retained.

How well are you conveying your message in more than one way?

Good Advice, Fast

"My father gave me the following advice on giving speeches —be sincere, be brief, be seated."
- James Roosevelt, son of U.S. President Franklin D. Roosevelt

We couldn't have said it better.

The Science of Stage Fright

When you get up to speak, your mouth goes dry, your palms get wet, and your stomach feels like lunch was a bad idea. What's wrong with you? Not a thing—it's how we're built.

Those feelings are caused by an almond-sized part of your brain called the amygdala. Research on rat brains in the 1980's revealed that the amygdala controls the expression of fear and anxiety. The amygdala appears to be at the center of most of the brain events associated with fear.

When you stand up to speak, your amygdala kicks into action. Here are some tips to control that anxiety:

- Breathe. Taking in oxygen causes the muscles to relax and eventually the brain gets the message that everything's okay.

- Look at one person at a time. Trying to take in the entire audience adds stimulation to your brain—and that's the last thing you need right now.

- Know what's happening. When you feel yourself getting nervous, acknowledge it to yourself and know that it's only your amygdala talking.

To See Or Not To See

If the eyes are the windows of the soul, what do you do when your audience can't see in? Presenters who wear glasses are faced with an unusual dilemma. Do they wear their glasses so they can see to read their script, or do they fly without them and risk bumping into furniture?

The answer really depends on whether you need them all the time or not. Many people who wear glasses can see well enough to present without, but wear them anyway. Reflections can make it difficult for the audience to see your eyes.

To see if you can work without them, try taking your glasses off before speaking in a meeting. Make good eye contact with everyone as you speak.

Just one more thought...don't underestimate the impact of putting your glasses on to read something during a presentation (gets their focus and can make you look professorial) or taking them off to make a point (it's an emphatic gesture, signaling great importance and allows you to look them squarely in the eye). Taking your glasses off might have dramatic results —look what it does for Superman!

Aggressive or Assertive?

As a presenter, do you want to seem aggressive, or do you want to seem assertive? The difference is important when trying to persuade an audience. Aggression is largely perceived as negative, while assertive behavior is perceived as positive. Here are some inherent behavior differences:

Aggressive conduct: Glares or stares at others
Assertive conduct: Makes friendly eye contact

Aggressive conduct: Intimidates others with body language
Assertive conduct: Shows confident body language that matches the message

Aggressive conduct: Has an air of inflexibility: "my way or the highway"
Assertive conduct: States one's needs, but genuinely considers other perspectives

Aggressive conduct: Considers other's perspectives only when demanded to do so
Assertive conduct: Considers other's perspectives without needing to be asked

Often when you try too hard to get your point across you can seem aggressive to your audience and undermine your effectiveness.

Understanding the difference from the audience's perspective is crucial. It's not what you mean to do, but how it appears to your audience that determines your ultimate success.

Don't Be a "Know-it-all"

"I can win an argument on any topic, against any opponent. People know this, and steer clear of me at parties. Often, as a sign of their great respect, they don't even invite me."

The American humor columnist Dave Barry makes a good point. "Know-it-alls" aren't terribly popular. Here are some tips for not sounding overbearing to your audience:

- Don't argue small points. Acknowledge that some people feel that way and move on.

- Ask the audience for examples rather than supplying them all yourself. This will also test their buy-in to your topic.

- Tell success stories that don't involve you. The fewer times you use the word "I," the less like an egomaniac you'll appear to your audience.

Answer Now or Later?

A common question among presenters is "Do I have participants hold all questions until the end of the presentation or answer them as they arise?" The answer depends on a number of factors:

- Will the question be a distraction to the listener and get in the way of their taking in new information? You may offer them the chance to ask a clarifying or informational question so that they will stay on track with you. If you're going to be covering that information, tell them so and ask their indulgence to hold the question until you've gotten to that subject.

- Will the question open a "can of worms" that could derail the presentation? Sometimes you can anticipate an audience's reaction. If you know it will be negative or emotional, you may want to hold all questions so you can present your evidence and supporting information. Then when you answer the questions you can tie the response to data you've already presented.

- How long will you be presenting? The longer a presenter speaks without interaction from the audience, the less likely he or she is to get them involved. A short presentation followed by lively Q and A is always better than a long presentation followed by silence from a benumbed audience.

Remember that how you handle questions from the audience may be their most lasting impression of you.

"Getting" Sarcasm

Have you ever wondered why some people never seem to "get" your jokes? It could be they are actually not physically able to process sarcasm.

A recent study at the University of Haifa in Israel used high-tech scanning equipment to track what happens in the brain when people were presented with sarcastic statements, such as "Hey Joe, don't work too hard," said to Joe when he was obviously relaxing. Some people recognized it as sarcasm and either laughed or became defensive, and others did not. Lack of response was most pronounced in autistic people with no discernable ability to process inconsistent messages.

What does this mean to you? It reminds you that when presenting, it might not be safe to assume that everyone will appreciate your witticisms. Inappropriate humor can backfire on a presenter. If you don't know how your audience will respond, don't take chances.

When in doubt, keep it positive.

Stand and Deliver

The moment you stand in front of an audience, they form an opinion of you. Scientists say first impressions are formed in less than three seconds. That's not a lot of time to win them over. Here are some tips for creating that positive first impression.

- Don't speak as you make your way to the front of the room. You don't want to draw attention to yourself as you dodge chairs or cords.

- Stand in a balanced position, both feet on the floor, hip width apart, hands at your side to start.

- Do not lean on the podium or table in front of you.

- Look the audience in the eye and smile before beginning your talk.

Fair or not, first impressions are hard to overcome. A good first impression makes your job as a communicator easier.

Another Reminder about Rehearsal

"That which we persist in doing becomes easier for us to do; not that the nature of the thing itself is changed, but that our power to do it is increased."
- Ralph Waldo Emerson

Just when you think we've quit nagging you about the power of rehearsal, we're back.

Presentation skills, like any physical behaviors, are a mix of habits and conscious skills. Practice volume, body language, and Eye-Brain Control, instead of merely flipping through the PowerPoint slides at your desk.

Everybody's Looking for a Handout...

If your handouts consist simply of your PowerPoint presentation with three slides to a page, you may be doing yourself a disservice.

When you confuse what the audience should take away with what you use to aid your stand-up presentation, you can wind up with visuals that distract from your presentation. If you simply give them your presentation, it may contain information they don't need (is the agenda slide really necessary?) or may not contain enough detail. It can also ruin a good surprise if they read ahead.

Here is a tip for making your handouts more effective without investing a lot more time than you can afford: copy only the slides they'll need into a separate file and print that.

- Expand the text, explain acronyms, and offer more complex reference material such as complete spread sheets or specs. It's not being projected so complexity is appropriate.

- Don't give your handout to the audience until you want them to have it. Often presenters say "they need something to make notes on." Provide legal pads or scratch paper and give them a clean version of the handout when you're done.

Controlling the distractions and increasing the impact of your handouts will only add to your credibility and your effectiveness as a presenter.

Give Out Cookies

Mark Katz, former speechwriter for U.S. President Bill Clinton, fights audience boredom by giving out verbal cookies. At least that's what he calls funny asides and planned humor.

In a recent interview, he told the reporter, "Any time someone gets up to give a speech, the audience assumes it's going to be bored. If you convince them otherwise, they'll sit up straighter and listen more intently." In order to prove them wrong, he suggests planning one humorous line per page of the speech. If the audience stays with you, they get a cookie (in the form of something not boring).

"Everyone likes cookies," he says, "even people on Atkins."

Red Dots and Playthings

Many presenters would be lost without their laser pointers or other hand-held props. Now they know how their audiences feel.

Most presenters who use laser pointers do so in order to guide their audience to a specific component of the visual they wish them to see. There are several problems with these tools:

- Most people cannot keep the little red dot still. It bounces around on the screen, causing more of a distraction than a help.

- By holding on to the pointer, the presenter has some thing in their hand they can play with. This becomes another source of distraction.

What can you do instead of using a laser pointer?

- *Use your hand.* Generally, what you are doing is showing the general part of the screen the audience should look at. Seldom do you have to be exact.

- *Direct the audience vocally.* A simple "in the top left quadrant" will tell the audience where you want them to look.

- *If it's that important, it should have its own visual.*

One of the reasons people use pointers is to pick an important piece of data out of a table, spreadsheet, or schematic. Simpler visuals let important information stand on its own. Don't fill the screen with clutter; the audience won't remember it anyway.

Taking—or Giving—Command?

Can you really develop "command" in someone with a poor presentation style such as soft voice or meek demeanor?

While some people are naturally more magnetic or effective presenters than others, it's important to keep in mind that qualities such as "credible" and "magnetic" are intangible qualities based on what people see and hear.

What an audience sees and hears is based on behaviors that we all exhibit and can improve. Vocal energy, eye contact, and rehearsal can help you create the perception of confidence, competence, and mastery of your material. Those behaviors can be modified, improved, and honed with practice and coaching.

The good news is that most of us can develop a decent level of skill. The bad news is that's seldom accomplished in a single session. True skill development requires a commitment to improvement that many individuals and organizations decide isn't worth the investment.

Add a Little Drama

Many business presentations have a routine. A slide appears, the presenter talks, and the next slide appears. Try spicing up your presentation with a little stage-craft to keep the audience engaged and a little surprised:

- Make an important point then hit the "B" button on your computer to make your screen go black. Tell them you want to remove any distractions and have them think about what you just said. Perhaps offer to take a few questions on that point before you move on.

- Walk forward with your eyes locked on the decision maker. This is a powerful move and conveys confidence and the importance of the moment.

- Drop your voice, rather than yell. This doesn't mean you suddenly become inaudible, but a change in tone makes your audience lean forward to hear, and you know you have their attention.

Teaching Charisma

In the journal *Personnel Psychology*, Annette J. Towler conducted research into whether or not "charisma" can be taught.

While she admits the research is sketchy, she did identify behaviors that leaders who create and motivate change, and who demonstrate "transformational leadership," most frequently exhibit when speaking:

- Articulating a vision: use of language that is emotionally appealing

- Appealing to followers' values: use of messages that appeal to social values of followers

- Use of autobiography: the use of personal history to reaffirm status as a role model

- Use of metaphors, analogies, and stories: examples of real-life incidents, metaphors, and analogies to give an emotional charge to their message

- Self-efficacy language: use of phrases that convey high expectations

While the scientific community is undecided on whether you can teach "charisma," we can certainly be more effective in using each of these techniques when developing motivational or change-oriented presentations to be more effective and bolster our image as a leader.

Writing and Speaking Aren't the Same Thing

"Speech and prose are not the same thing. They have different wavelengths, for speech moves at the speed of light, where prose moves at the speed of the alphabet, and must be consecutive and grammatical and word-perfect. Prose cannot gesticulate. Speech can sometimes do nothing more."

- James Kenneth Stephens (1882-1950), Irish poet and author

Here's another reason not to write speeches word-for-word. Phrases that look great on paper may sound awkward when read aloud. We couldn't have said it better ourselves.

Eye-Brain Control in the Dark

How do you exhibit good "Eye-Brain Control" when you are in front of a large crowd in a darkened auditorium?

That question comes up a lot. When you can't clearly see the faces of the people in your audience, it's easy to slip into old habits. Here are some tips for working a large crowd:

- Start with the people you *can* see. Usually these are in the front rows. This will enable you to gauge where "eye-level" is for the rest of the group.

- Work different parts of the room. It looks more natural and allows you to keep the maximum number of people engaged.

- Even though you can't see them, they can see you clearly. Look directly to where you know their eyes are. Don't give in to the temptation to talk to the back wall.

What You and Bill Gates Have in Common

Most presenters who use technology like PowerPoint or the web to present have nightmares about the day it just doesn't work during an important presentation. One of the most famous instances happened (through bad luck or divine justice depending on your viewpoint) to Bill Gates, the founder of Microsoft.

On a public stage, with literally the whole world watching, he began a presentation on Microsoft's (then) new Windows 98 platform— and the only thing that appeared on screen was the ominous message "fatal exception error." At least if your presentation goes bust, it won't show up on the evening news.

What did Gates do at that moment? Exactly what any presenter should do in that situation:

- Keep a sense of humor

- See if you can fix it yourself quickly; if not, get help before you waste too much time

- Cover what you can until it's fixed

- Reboot and cross your fingers

Presenting is not easy, and when you add variables such as technology, distance, or audience size, it can be exponentially more complex. The good news is that it needn't make your presentation a "fatal exception error." It needn't be fatal at all.

Stay calm, have a backup plan and know your information.

Questions about Q & A

One of the most common questions speakers ask is, "How can I look calm and under control during Question and Answer time when I'm scared to death?"

Remember, what goes on between your ears is of no concern to your audience—they will respond to what they see and hear. Here are some cues that let the audience think you have it all under control:

- *Take your time answering.* Few things in life are as unnerving as not answering the question properly, or worse, answering the wrong question. Take the time to listen, understand the issue, and take a deep breath before answering.

- *Balance up.* Many presenters do well covering their nervousness by balancing their stance and looking their audience in the eye, but when Q and A comes they are so concentrated on giving the best answer that they forget about the physical skills. The most articulate answer can be undermined and appear evasive if you're swaying or playing with a ring on your finger.

- *Finish your thoughts.* One of the most common habits presenters have when answering questions is to let their thoughts trail off. This can make them look unconfident in their answer and start the next question with low energy. Try having a summary statement in the back of your mind like "So, that's why I say..." so that you can finish with a declarative sentence, and not a whimper.

Transitioning Between Visuals

Whether presenting at the front of the room, or during a webinar, presenters sometimes get into a pattern of saying the same thing as they change visuals. An audience can only take so much "And on this next slide you'll see..." before their eyes start to roll.

Taking a moment to plan your transitions will make you appear more spontaneous and professional. This is particularly true of webinars, when people have limited attention spans.

Some smooth transitions are:

- Preview the next topic ("Now that we've talked about ____ let's look at____")

- Silence

- Checking in for a response ("_____, does that match your experience?")

- A short factoid or additional information ("By the way, did you know...")

Quote from the Master

Here's a quote you should keep in mind:

"Formulate and stamp indelibly on your mind a mental picture of yourself as succeeding. Hold this picture tenaciously. Never permit it to fade. Your mind will seek to develop the picture. Do not build up obstacles in your imagination."

- Dale Carnegie

In other words, take a moment before presenting to imagine yourself giving your presentation perfectly, rather than obsessing about what could go wrong. It may seem like stating the obvious, but it remains good advice.

If anyone would know, it's Dale Carnegie. His book, *How to Win Friends and Influence People*, is a classic of business and personal success writing and still sells hundreds of thousands of copies a year.

Toastmasters

If you ever think you're alone in your stage fright or concern about your speaking skills, here's something that will make you feel better.

Toastmasters International recently celebrated its 81st year of helping people learn to speak more effectively in public. Here are some stats that should let you know you're in good company:

- They have 195,000 members worldwide

- There are 9,300 clubs

- A scientific base in Antarctica has a sanctioned club, making it the only organization in the world with charter members on all seven continents

- Over 80 countries have official Toastmaster clubs

Joining Toastmasters is a great way to keep the skills Communispond teaches sharp and effective.

For information on how to find Toastmasters clubs near you, visit www.toastmasters.org.

Lessons from Grade School

You may find yourself nostalgic for the days of your youth, but there's one thing you probably don't miss—Show and Tell.

Here are some similarities between that childhood rite of passage and business presentations:

- *It's nerve-wracking.* Studies of elementary students say "Show and Tell" is one of kids' least favorite activities.

- *The shorter the better.* Kids who stay up there too long tend to ramble and don't know how to end their presentations. Sound like anyone you know?

- *Don't bring anything you can't handle.* You wouldn't bring something for show and tell that would break, create a mess, or get away and scare the teacher unless you really knew what you were doing. Same thing applies, whether it's your pet frog or unfamiliar presentation technology.

The more things change, the more they stay the same.

Could You Pass "The Apprentice" Test?

Not that we're out to advertise a TV show, but have you noticed how often success or failure on the NBC television show, *The Apprentice*, hinges on the final presentation?

In the 2005 season of the show, final presentations were the key factor in the contestants' success or failure. Not surprisingly, those who did well continued, while at least four participants in the show were "fired" after giving weak presentations. In one case, a participant did not feel confident enough to present.

Donald Trump himself has said on several occasions, "I don't need anyone in my organization who won't step up to present."

More and more, your perception in your company is based on the face you present to others and your willingness to step up—even if you don't work for Donald Trump.

Give a Presentation and Kill Germs

If you worry about the stress of giving a presentation, here's some news that will make you feel better. Giving a presentation can actually kill germs that cause infections.

We understand that this one requires an explanation. According to research at the University of British Columbia, the short-term stress of giving a presentation causes the body to create hormones and other chemicals that not only make you nervous and edgy, they also strengthen your immune system.

Apparently the body equates the stress of public speaking with that of a cold or other mild infection, and rises to the occasion. So don't think of it as having to give a presentation; think of it as preventative medicine.

Using Your Powers for Good...

"Can there be a more horrible object in existence than an eloquent man not speaking the truth?"
- Thomas Carlyle

Thomas Carlyle reminds us of the power of effective speaking. He was saying that when someone uses all the tools of effective persuasion to convince the audience of something they know isn't true, great mischief can be the result.

On the other hand, he could have said if you want to tell the truth, and use all your powers of persuasion, there is no more positive power.

The good news is that the skills necessary to become "eloquent" (powerful delivery, and strong organization of thought and logic), are skills that are teachable and can be mastered with practice. That's what we are committed to at Communispond.

Imagine if all of us could tell the truth as eloquently as we are sometimes told things that are not true.

"Great Moments in Communication"

1847 TO OVERCOME DIFFICULTIES IN BRINGING COLLEAGUES TO A MEETING TO DISCUSS SHIPPING PRACTICES, CAPTAIN HANSON GREGORY INVENTS THE DOUGHNUT

Audiences

It's Who You Know...

Don't you love when they invent something that helps you do something you should have done all along?

In a recent press release, a company announced that it is introducing electronic nametags for people who attend conferences. Besides flashing your name and where you're from, it also captures contact information from the person you're speaking to and what vendor needs they may have. Finally, the network meets, well, networking.

Even without the high-tech wizardry, the power of meeting the members of your audience and establishing their specific needs and objectives before you speak cannot be overemphasized. It allows you to do a number of things:

- It reduces nervousness by personalizing your audience; calling an individual by name is less intimidating than facing a nameless crowd.

- It humanizes you in the eyes of the audience. People tend to be more respectful of people they've connected with.

- Using names and information you have just gleaned prior to the presentation helps your credibility ("Joe, you mentioned before we started that you have a problem with turnover…")

- You can tailor your presentation "on the fly" to focus on the needs of your audience.

- You also get to do something besides obsess about your presentation. Your nervousness will be reduced and your brain constructively occupied if you're not just sitting in a corner looking scared and talking to yourself.

Even if you don't have a high-tech gizmo to help, get out there and mingle with your audience before a presentation and see the difference it makes.

Audiences Don't Like New Ideas

If you are surprised at the resistance your ideas receive sometimes, don't feel bad. Many audiences feel like the person who made this quote: "I will ignore all ideas for new works on engines of war, the invention of which has reached its limits and for whose improvements I see no further hope."

Here's the amazing part. That was said in A.D. 80 by the Roman Sextus Julius Frontinus. What more could there be to learn, then?

Persuasion sometimes starts by remembering where your audience is starting, rather than where you want them to go, or they may feel like there's nothing really new.

Establish a Presentation Contract

One way to keep your audience engaged from the beginning is to tell them what they're in for. Mike Feiner, a professor at the Columbia Graduate School of Business and author of *The Feiner Points of Leadership*, says to establish a "presentation contract" right at the beginning.

Telling the audience what to expect from you and what you expect from them helps reduce the "why am I here?" questions that sometimes occur, and lets them know that this is not a passive experience—their feedback, questions, or challenges are a scheduled part of the program.

"The contract basically says, 'Here's what I'm going to talk about, here's what you ought to expect of me,'" he told *Jungle* magazine. The challenge, as you can imagine, is then living up to what you've promised.

Avoid Overloading the Audience

Have you ever felt like your brain is too full to take in new information, so that you just tune out? It turns out that it is temporarily full. Knowing why this happens can help you avoid overloading your audience and help them remember key components of your presentation.

Numerous studies going as far back as the 1950s indicate that our brain has two sets of memory: long-term and short-term. Information goes to short-term memory first, then with time and processing, into long-term storage. The problem is our short-term memory can only store seven (give or take a couple) pieces of new information at a time. Without time to process, new information may not enter, or older information may get pushed out, just like holding a full waterglass under the tap.

So how do you make this work for you?

- *Very carefully* decide what points are most important for the audience to retain. Make several cuts at the information, using a forced-choice process.

- *Save details* for the handouts.

- *Don't hold Q & A* until the end of their presentation. Allowing people to process information in small doses clears up short-term memory and allows them to remember more of the total presentation.

Attention... Don't Forget the Snacks

Want to increase the attention span of your audience? Don't underestimate the importance of the goodies at the back of the room.

According to Dr. Joseph Mercola, author of *The Total Health Program*, one of the biggest factors affecting a person's ability to focus on a task of presentation is the amount of sugar in their system. And for those of you on diets, sugar does *not* mean the snacks have to be unhealthy.

"Low blood sugar (hypoglycemia), can occur when otherwise healthy individuals neglect to eat, and can slow the speed at which people process information and shorten their attention span," Dr. Mercola explains. Although low blood sugar can be reversed with just a few bites of a sandwich, it can affect daily activities at work and at home.

Explain that to your finance people next time they want to cut the budget for doughnuts.

Removing Electronic Distractions

Does your audience sometimes seem to be more interested in their email and text messages than in your presentation? Here are some tips to subtly, and obviously, remove distractions.

- Make a show of turning off your cell phone or text device just before you speak. This will cue others to do the same.

- Start by acknowledging the pressures of the outside world. Let your audience know how long you'll be speaking and why they should stay involved.

- Ask questions of people in the audience and call on people by name if possible. If they know they're expected to respond they are more likely to stay focused on you.

- Ask the person who is hosting the meeting to make an announcement. The audience is more likely to listen to their manager than to an outside party.

At Last, a Place to Use Your Geometry

Ever wonder how you'd use your high school geometry? Try using it during a presentation to a large audience.

By focusing on the eyes of one person in a large audience, you'll make others feel like you're talking directly to them. The reason is geometric. Your gaze focuses on a single point, but your angle serves as the tip of a triangle. Everyone in that triangular view will experience the feeling of you looking at them.

This is much more effective than finding a spot on the back of the wall, or looking over their heads as some people recommend.

Now you'll be able to tell your kids there is a use for geometry in the real world.

Don't Fight Your Audience

It's important to analyze your audience. The key is to overcome our own preferences, and focus on what the audience wants. Here are some things to help keep you on track:

- Even if you are endlessly fascinated by detail, resist the urge to tell them that one last interesting fact, if you suspect the only person interested is you.

- Anticipate their questions. If it becomes apparent that they want to know mainly about implementation, plan to spend most of your time discussing this subject.

- If you are bored with small details but know your audience will want them, prepare the information as a handout so you can refer to it and satisfy their curiosity.

Analyzing your audience doesn't do you any good unless you're prepared to make the changes dictated by that analysis. Don't fight it, and the results will be worth the work.

Degrees of Change

An audience's willingness to act on your recommendations frequently depends on the degree of change you're recommending. In other words, your audience's response hinges on how crucial your audience thinks the problem is and how dire the consequences.

The three degrees of change are:

1. "We could be doing this better." Things are working, but things could be improved. This is hard to get people to buy into because it requires change, and the advantages of your recommendation aren't always clear.

2. "If we don't fix this, we're in trouble." The problem is now apparent, and the consequences of not taking

action are obvious. This is often the easiest to get people to buy into, although it elevates the stress level and can complicate implementation.

3. "It's a major crisis." The problem is big, and we're already suffering the consequences. By this time, options may be limited and people aren't thinking clearly, but they have to do something.

If you're going to get people to take action, how you approach them will depend on the degree of change you're asking them to make.

Are People in the Middle Smarter?

Recent university studies show that presenters and teachers tend to overestimate the abilities of people in the middle of a group over people at the outside edges. Perhaps this is because people in the middle tend to arrive early, giving the appearance of eagerness.

Maybe it's because they haven't positioned themselves for an early exit, and therefore are more engaged.

Either way, as presenters, we should: a) be aware of this tendency and double-check our assumptions about the audience, and b) pick that middle spot if we want to be taken more seriously when others are presenting to us.

Trade Show Presenting

Trade show audiences are a special case for presenters. How do you present effectively to noisy crowds of people as they hurry from one exhibit to the next?

If you're presenting one-on-one:

- Try taking the person deeper into the booth, out of the way of traffic

- Since time is limited, determine the person's main interests

- Target your presentation, instead of giving a "canned" features-and-benefits speech

If you're presenting to a group:

- Keep the presentation short

- Try to get them out of the traffic and into chairs; they're tired and would love the chance to sit

- If at all possible, let them get their hands on the product or demo

Remember, at any trade show, the majority of people are just looking. Try and focus on those few leads or prospects that will get results rather than try to cover everyone.

Humor and Gender

Stanford University research shows that men and women find humor in different things. Besides saving marriages, how is this information useful to presenters?

When presenting, it's important to remember that humor can help warm up an audience and make your ideas more acceptable, but one size does not fit all. Think carefully about your audience and how they will react. It might not be the same way you do.

The study showed that while watching cartoons, women activated the left prefrontal cortex more than men, indicating that they process humor more through language than through visual humor. Men find more humor in the visual areas of the brain.

Depending on your audience, that same pun or cartoon may not be the best idea for your next presentation.

Positive Messages–Positive Results

A recent university study shows that when you send positive body signals, you'll appear more favorable to your audience—and maybe even convince yourself.

A study at Ohio State University, published in *Discover* magazine, used 82 college students to listen to two messages. One group exhibited non-verbal approval signals like smiling and nodding, the other frowned and shook their heads. One message was a logical argument for a simple topic; the other made the same point but with more dubious logic.

Nodders and smilers were more likely than the control group to agree with the persuasive message, but actually less likely to concur with the weaker argument. Nodding apparently boosted the subects' confidence in their assessment of the situation.

It appears our actions influence not only emotions but our beliefs and attitudes as well.

For speakers, this is important information—watch your audience's reactions. Model nodding and other positive non-verbal behaviors when you interact with people in order to encourage the same.

The Right Brain and Gestures

People who talk more with their hands tend to be "right-brained." Studies at several universities show that people who are "left-brained" (primarily logical and linear in their thinking) use their hands to gesture and speak less than people who are right-brained (who tend to think in pictures or concepts).

No one is quite sure why, although one general theory is that when you think of a word like "big," the right-brained person has a more physical reaction: it's natural to try to show "big" with their body to demonstrate the concept. In fact, when their hands are restrained, many people who naturally talk with their hands are almost incapable of speech at all.

This is another reason why gestures are so important to communicate to an audience. Besides making your physical appearance more interesting, they can help left-brained people engage right-brainers, and right-brained people understand a concept so they can then explain it more logically to left-brainers.

Either way, controlled, appropriate gestures help you communicate your ideas more effectively regardless of your audience.

Tips From a Hypnotist

Here's a lesson in audience control from Communispond's book, *The Full Force of Your Ideas—Mastering the Science of Persuasion.*

The technique is based on the work of hypnotist Milton Erickson, who believed you could more quickly work up a rapport with a subject (or an audience) by what he called "Pacing and Leading."

In a nutshell, this means matching the audience or subject's energy level and body language, then leading them in the direction you wish to go.

Let's say the audience is hyper and distracted. If you start at a low energy level, you might not capture them. On the other hand, if they are reserved and quiet, and you start too loud and boisterous you might alienate them before you even have them.

Once you match their energy level, you can then vary your own energy up or down as necessary, as you'll have established a rapport.

Take a moment to test your audience; meet them where they are, and they'll be more willing to follow you.

Fighting Demo Distraction

People who demonstrate equipment or products are faced with audiences that are often distracted. How do you keep their attention?

- Acknowledge what's around them to satisfy their curiosity ("There's a lot to look at and we'll get to it...").

- Tie your demo to their needs ("You said you wanted to see... and this will...").

- Draw their attention to the matter at hand, and quote them if you can ("This will do exactly what you said you needed...").

- Keep it short.

By clearly stating what you're going to do and acknowledging possible distractions, you'll be able to focus attention on the matter at hand, at least momentarily.

The "Magic Number" and Why We Care About It

Have you ever listened to a presentation and felt like your brain was full and couldn't take in one more piece of information? It was, and you couldn't.

In 1956, Dr. George Miller determined the "magic number" of pieces of information people could take in at one time. He determined it was 7 + 2. That's why U.S. local phone numbers are seven digits long; it's all you can keep in your head without writing it down.

There is only so much data an audience can accept without a chance to process the information, either through discussion, questioning, or simply giving them a break.

A data dump is not only frustrating, it simply doesn't work. Now you know why.

Audience Body Language Matters

New scientific evidence proves what we've always known intuitively—audience response can affect whether you think you do your job well or not.

A study at Texas Christian University was conducted by comparing professor self-assessments and job satisfaction with end-of-course student assessments. Then they analyzed the differences:

- 26 % of the variation in their self-assessment was based on verbal and non-verbal feedback from participants

- 53% of teachers' job satisfaction came from the responses of class participants

Interestingly, the study also showed that the professors gave nonverbal communication (body language and facial expressions) more weight than verbal responses.

Handling Objections

"It is a thing of no great difficulty to raise objections against another man's oration, nay, it is a very easy matter; but to produce a better in its place is a work extremely troublesome."
- Plutarch (A.D 100 or so)

We present this to you for two reasons:

1. It might make you feel better to know that no matter how brilliant your presentation, someone will find fault with it

2. It's been going on for thousands of years

Try this useful tactic: put yourself in their seats for a moment and try to anticipate possible objections. They'll still come, but at least you'll be ready for them.

Presenting to Mixed Groups

It's easy to say, "Just analyze your audience and give them what's important to them." What if you have a diverse audience, with mixed levels of knowledge about your subject?

- *Acknowledge the mix of attendees.* People will be more patient if they know that a majority of the audience doesn't have the information they do.

- *Give them a reason to care.* Sometimes mixed groups don't understand why a piece of information may be important or how it relates to them. Try to tie it to the various constituencies: "For those of you in IT this is important because…"

- *Time goes to the decision maker.* In cases where you have limited time, focus on the decision maker, and let everyone know that's what you're doing. Other attendees understand that and will be less willing to hold you up, if only so they don't appear unknowledgeable in front of the boss.

Argumentative Audiences

It's one thing to deal with an audience member who disagrees with you, but it's even worse when things start to turn nasty. How do you deal with argumentative audience members?

- Find out what the issue is. Most often, there is some concern about the topic or the data that is driving this negative behavior. Before you try to argue facts, find out what the real concern is.

- Keep language neutral. Rephrase the challenge, removing the argumentative language. Keep the conversation on the issue, not the personalities.

- *Find out if it's just them.* How you ultimately handle
  it depends on whether argumentative individuals speak
  only for themselves or represent a larger challenge. Poll
  the audience to find out if the same challenge exists for
  them. If it does, you'll have to address it. If it doesn't
  apply to anyone but the challenger, offer to take it off-
  line so as to make the best use of the group's time.

The New Brain

Does it seem like younger audiences think differently
than older ones? Recent scientific evidence suggests there may
be a biological reason for that.

According to neuropsychiatrist Richard Restak, in his
book, *The New Brain*, evolution may be catching up to modern technology. The old belief has been that people are less
effective while trying to do two things at once—for example,
read a book and watch television. Studies show that an increasing number of people under 30, though, are able to excel
while taking in multiple messages. While these savants are still
in the minority among people under 30, they are almost double the proportion of those over 30 with that capability, indicating that our biology may be changing to meet the demands
of the 21st century.

As communicators, we need to be prepared to deliver
our message in a number of ways so that the multimedia gen-
eration will get it. Remember to look at age in your audience
analysis.

"Great Moments in Communication"

2670 BC HEMON, VIZIER TO PHAROH KHUFU, INVENTS THE VISUAL AID IN ORDER TO OVERCOME A CONSTRUCTION PROBLEM ON THE GREAT PYRAMID

Presentation Content

So Get Started Already

> *"You can't wait for inspiration. You have to go after it with a club."*
>
> - Jack London, U.S. adventurer, author, & sailor (1876 - 1916)

Let's face it, when planning a presentation the hardest part is waiting for inspiration. Unfortunately, we can't all wait for the brilliant idea or we'd be staring at a blank sheet of paper all day. Here are some tips to draw inspiration out of its hiding place:

- Try starting with your point. Say to your audience, "When I'm finished today, I'd like you to..." and tell them why.

- Don't open PowerPoint until you know what you're going to say. That first blank slide is just depressing.

- Doodle and Mind-Map. This is a great way to "brain storm" by yourself.

Inspiration is hard to come by, but it can be tracked down with a little work. Happy hunting!

Define Your Outcome

Here's the simplest way to focus your presentation and make sure you're on track. Before you present, determine the benefit to your audience by finishing this statement:

"At the end of this presentation I want the audience to..."

If you want them to know something, you can limit your information to just that. If you want them to do something, let them know what it is right up front.

This is also a great way to beat writer's block. Just tell your audience what you want to accomplish, and they'll help you get there.

Don't Plan in PowerPoint

Here's a piece of advice that may seem counter-intuitive: Don't use PowerPoint or other software packages to plan your presentation. Plan first, then use the software to build a presentation that really sings.

Many of us open PowerPoint and start filling in blank slides in the order they come up in the template we've chosen. The problem is that these templates, while well-meaning, are designed to create generic, cookie-cutter presentations. Is that what you're really trying to achieve? Great presentations start with knowing what you want to accomplish, who your audience is, and the most powerful and concise way to get that message across. You need to know all those things before sitting down to fill in a template.

By knowing what you want to accomplish you can:

- Choose the most appropriate visuals and format for your audience—senior management probably doesn't need to see an orange fireball on every screen

- Make wiser decisions about how to organize your information

- Remove unnecessary slides to keep your presentation as lean and powerful as possible

By taking the time to plan your presentation before building it, you will be able to use the tools to greater effect and get your message across better than ever.

Grab Them Quickly

Which of these sentences grabs your attention?

- "Sales are up dramatically"
- "Sales are up 10% over last year"
- "Sales are up $2 million over this time last year"

For most audiences it will be the last one. Why?

- Grabbers speak to the individual's experience. We know what $2 million is, even if we'll never see it.

- Grabbers are specific—real numbers are more engaging than "a lot" or "substantially."

- Grabbers change for each audience. If you are an investor, that 10% might be a more important number than the $2 million.

Grab your audience with the opening sentence.

The Last Should Be First

Here's a unique way to get to the point of your presentation quickly—put the last slide first.

What do we mean?

Many of us build our presentations so that they lead to a single recommendation or solution. By taking your recommendation slide and moving it to the front, you have gotten to the point of your presentation and the rest of the information then supports that recommendation. Odds are you'll use fewer slides, too.

So if you insist on using PowerPoint to build your presentation, get all your ideas down, then take the next step—use the "last slide first" technique to whittle it down to an audience-friendly final version.

Signal-to-Noise Ratio

In physics, there is a lot of talk about the signal-to-noise ratio. In short, it measures the clarity of a signal; the less noise, the more clearly understood the signal, and the less chance the rocket will go off course. How does this apply to us as presenters?

Think of the signal as that information that is of value to your audience: facts, numbers, application. Noise is the information that makes the signal less clear or distracts from your message. It's extraneous information, made up of facts with no context, so the audience doesn't know or care how it applies to them. Noise can also be just too much detail for your audience to process.

Our messages need more signal and less noise.

Data or Wisdom?

According to organizational change expert Russell Ackoff, when we tell an audience something, it's not necessarily information. He offers a hierarchy of the kinds of things you can communicate, starting with data:

- *Data:* symbols, numbers, graphs

- *Information:* data is processed and put in context; provides answers to "who," "what," "where," and "when" questions

- *Knowledge:* applies the data and information; answers "how" questions

- *Understanding:* appreciation of "why" the listener should care

- *Wisdom:* evaluated understanding and the most persuasive and useful application of the data

Colorful Charts Help—a Little

Software that creates pie charts, line graphs, and other visuals is extremely helpful to those of us who build presentations. We should also be careful that we do our audience a service as well.

Here are some tips for making sure that the colors you use will enhance the audience's retention and not be a distraction:

- *Do not rely on templates.* Choose colors that are easy on the eyes. Make sure that explanatory text like legends are readable, even if it means changing the defaults that the software provides.

- *Make sure that there is a match between the color and the message.* For example, in Western culture, red is usually reserved for bad news. In the U.S., green is associated with good financial news.

- *Whatever color you're using, make sure it's legible when projected.* What looks fine projected on your desktop may wash out or look different when projected on a screen. This is particularly true of yellow and green.

The point of visuals is to support your data, not dazzle your audience. Never let them become a distraction.

What is Your Audience Thinking?

Presenters are always looking for ways to communicate their points to reluctant audiences. The simplest answer may come by asking yourself, "What does my audience think it needs?" rather than "What do I think they need to know?"

By making this minor shift in thinking, you won't overwhelm your audience with data and background. Instead, you'll move to address the one burning question you have as an audience member: "What am I doing here and why should I care?"

Answering that question first will give your audience a reason to listen. It will almost certainly shorten your presentation, and keep you from putting too much information up front.

Is Logic More Powerful than Poetry?

According to former White House speechwriter Peggy Noonan, the logic of a speech is more moving than flowery words or poetry. Her example is a good one: Lincoln's Gettysburg Address.

At the dedication of a memorial for the war dead at Gettysburg, Lincoln was to speak. The person before him, a famed orator named Edward Everett, spoke for two hours, pulling out all the stops. He used poetry, classical references, the most emotion-wrenching words he could think of. Lincoln then got up and spoke for two or three minutes—words that still echo years later.

According to Noonan, in the book *Simply Speaking*, the reason it was so powerful is the logic of the speech. Put simply, Lincoln:

- Defined the meaning of the war

- Put it into historical context

- Showed the country that he understood the drama of the last three years

"It was a speech about the thinking of the president. It contained the logic of the war. In time people understood how beautiful it was, and were moved by it and learned it by heart," she says. "But again, it became these things because it was a thoughtful speech, a speech that defined things. Its logic was moving."

Make sure the logic of your presentation is solid, and powerful things will happen.

Emotions = Memories

A university study has confirmed what most of us already know. Images that appeal to our emotions remain with us longer. This is something to consider in your next presentation.

The study's authors presented ten healthy male volunteers with a series of pictures. Some of the images were meant to evoke pleasant or unpleasant responses, such as pictures with sexual or gastronomic appeal. Some pictures were of neutral subjects like plants and rooms. Others were thought to have little or no emotional impact, such as a picture of a chrome rhinoceros, or an exotic festival.

Four weeks later, the men were quizzed on their memory of the various pictures. The authors report that "long-term...recognition memory was substantially enhanced for the pleasant, aversive, and interesting pictures relative to the neutral pictures."

Think about this the next time you're putting together yet another bulleted list.

Organizing By Rubric

A rubric is not a cube, and it's not somebody's name. It is an imposing word that means "a short commentary or explanation covering a broad topic." It's a common term in academic circles, but even those of us who aren't college professors can use it effectively.

Break a seemingly broad presentation into headings, and group them by sub-topic. You'll quickly discover which points can be included under another category, which can be grouped together, and which you can do without.

Your subheadings now make a great agenda slide for your presentation, setting your audience's expectations while keeping you on task.

Get Thee To a Thesaurus

"Words are not as satisfactory as we should like them to be, but, like our neighbours, we have got to live with them and must make the best and not the worst of them."
- Samuel Butler, English author 1835-1902

The words we use when presenting are not exact tools, but the more precise we can be, the better the end result. For this reason, we suggest "making the best of them" by being as exact as you can be:

- *Don't overuse a word.* Find synonyms that work. The word "prerequisite," for example, also means "need," "requirement," or "qualification."

- *Be precise.* If something is "mandatory," it's not simply "important."

- *Be colorful.* Use a thesaurus to find words that paint a picture. You don't have to be pretentious, but use words that are out of the ordinary to grab your listeners' attention.

Ten-Dollar Words

Here's a quote from comedian George Carlin that sums up what your audience often thinks of your message: "The more syllables a euphemism has, the further divorced from reality it is."

Think twice about using a fancy word for what you're trying to say. Your audience is neither fooled nor impressed.

Color Your Words

Would you rather receive a compliment or bask in one? Are you angry at someone or livid? Maybe you're spitting nails, you're so furious.

The words we choose can convey not only our message, but shades of emotion, meaning, and other "color" beyond mere definitions. When building your presentation, try to think of a couple of "colorful" words to involve your audience.

Many of us try to keep the language in business presentations neutral, but sometimes passion and emotion are important to achieve buy-in or get the attention of people who aren't aware of how strongly you feel.

In the words of John Maynard Keynes: "Words ought to be a little wild, for they are the assault of thoughts on the unthinking."

Similes and Metaphors

We all learned about similes and metaphors in primary school, but do you know how they can make your presentations more engaging and effective? Do you know the difference between a simile and a metaphor?

Simile compares two things with at least one common trait, usually containing the words "like" or "as," for example: "My love is like a red, red rose." Exactly how it's like a rose is up to the author.

Metaphor relates two things that may not have something obvious in common. A metaphor generally says something is something else, instead of comparing it: "This country is a shining city on a hill." A country is obviously not a city—unless you live in Monte Carlo—but it makes a point.

Both help explain technical or controversial topics in language the audience can relate to emotionally.

Why Are You Updating People?

Project updates can be a complete bore for an audience. As a presenter, you can fix that. It's important in the planning and organizing stage of your presentation to ask yourself some questions:

- What is the audience expected to do with this information?

- Do you have to present the information in the same way each time?

- Which piece of the project is most impacted, and do they know why?

- Is there a clear reason to communicate the impact on the project?

Why put everyone through it if nothing can be gained by meeting? Adjust the meeting according to the answers to these questions, and keep people engaged and interested.

Use Those Building Blocks

Not every audience is the same, and not every presentation will have the same impact. The key is to look at the building blocks of your presentation. Here are some tips:

- Use only four to five building blocks for a presentation.

- Start with an attention-grabber tailored for your audience. Every presentation should start with why the audience should listen.

- Not all building blocks are the same length; the shorter the better. Save the details, and concentrate on the elements of interest for your audience.

Giving and Getting Advice

Does your audience overvalue advice when the problem is critical, and undervalue it when they don't see a threat? According to *Harvard Business Review*, that's not unusual.

Research by Francesca Gino shows that decision makers overvalue advice when a problem is hard, and undervalue it when the solution seems clear. They also tend to overvalue advice from external consultants versus internal stakeholders.

What does this mean to us as presenters?

- Does your audience truly understand the gravity of the situation you're trying to address?

- Have you established your credibility to speak to the issue under discussion?

- Do you know the stakes for your audience?

Making yourself a resource to decision makers is a vital step to project (and career) success.

Advice from Linus Pauling

Nobel Prize winner Linus Pauling had this advice for his students: "The key to creativity is to have lots and lots of ideas, then throw away the bad ones."

Whether you're trying to break new ground in bio-chemistry or update the project team, take the time to brain-storm and generate lots of ideas before creating your presentation, then throw out the ideas that don't work. It's a whole lot easier than trying to get the only idea you've got to come out coherently.

Shooting for the "Soundbite"

All of us who give presentations long to create the perfect "soundbite"—that short, pithy, memorable quote that will stay with the audience long after the presentation is over.

Peggy Noonan, who helped write some of Ronald Reagan's greatest speeches and is considered one of the modern masters of the art form, had this to say about the quest for the perfect quotable nugget:

"Great speeches have always had great soundbites. The problem now is that the young technicians who put together speeches are paying attention only to the soundbite, not to the text as a whole, not realizing that all great soundbites happen by accident, which is to say, all great soundbites are yielded up inevitably, as part of the natural expression of the text. They are part of the tapestry, they aren't a little flower somebody sewed on." (*What I Saw at the Revolution*, 1990)

In other words, plan your whole presentation well, pay attention to the details, and the soundbites will appear naturally. Don't force it.

Letting People More Famous Than You Make Your Point...

"Whenever I see a young man make a great presentation, I never forget that young man. Unfortunately the opposite is also true."
- Jack Welch

Do we have your attention? Using an authority or famous person to back up your point of view is often a good idea. Start your presentation with a quote from a famous person or recognized expert in your field.

Where do you find these pithy words of wisdom? Online resources are plentiful. One of the most accessible and useful is www.bartlebys.com, which offers a classic edition of *Bartlett's Quotations* and a wealth of sources. Or if you're so inclined, visit www.insults.net.

Be careful. As George Bernard Shaw said, "If you're going to tell people the truth, make them laugh or they'll kill you."

Top Speeches Point Toward the Future

The web site "American Rhetoric" has listed the top 100 speeches in recent American history. We found it interesting that the top three share a common theme—the future. The three speeches are:

- "I Have a Dream" speech by Martin Luther King, Jr.

- John F. Kennedy's First Inaugural Address

- Franklin Delano Roosevelt's First Inaugural Address

All three are brilliant speeches, delivered by different men with different styles. Here are some things they have in common:

- They point to a possible, positive (although not easily achieved) future

- They use "we" language frequently when mentioning the solution, rather than "me" or "you"

- They acknowledge the difficulties of achieving their goals

Think about that the next time you're planning a presentation that tackles big goals.

For a full list, visit Top 100 American Speeches: http://www.americanrhetoric.com/top100speechesall.html.

A New 80-20 Rule

At Communispond, we've always said that planning is vital to the creation of an effective presentation. Here's another way to look at it. Eighty percent of your preparation time should be spent planning and strategizing your presentation rather than building it in PowerPoint.

We spend a lot of time worrying about our PowerPoint slides or creating pretty visuals. If we keep our presentation concise by thinking about our audience and focusing on those points that will create the most value to our listeners, our presentation will take less time to build. Moreover, it will hit the mark better than if we use the software to build our presentation as we go.

Analogies Only Work When Your Audience Can Relate to Them...

Ever heard a speaker use sports analogies? "A Hail Mary pass" is a last-ditch effort to accomplish something. To "know where the puck is going, instead of where it's been" is to anticipate changes in the environment and be proactive. They're great analogies for common themes...if you understand them.

In today's business environment it's important to understand that your audience may not see the world as you do. People of varying backgrounds make up your audience, and your job is to make sure you speak to them as clearly as possible.

For example, the use of sports (particularly North American sports) or military analogies can alienate people who don't participate in those sports, who have strong feelings about the military, or who don't share your cultural background. Try mixing it up—cooking, popular entertainment, and the daily newspaper offer lots of alternatives to tired clichés.

Know your audience and adjust to their needs—you'll be seen as much more effective.

Keep Something for Later

One way to keep your presentations short, and add to your credibility during Q & A, is to keep valuable information that supports your point of view in reserve and close at hand.

When editing your presentation, try pulling out one valuable—but not essential—example, story, or statistic and keeping it close at hand. You can anticipate the most common audience questions. When the audience asks the question, as you know they will, you can say, "I'm glad you asked that..." and voila. You look prepared, competent, and extremely credible.

If you're using flip charts or white boards for this value-added information, know what you want to put up there in advance and practice. Spelling and money calculations are tough to do without practice.

If you're using PowerPoint, add a couple of charts or graphs at the end of your presentation (past the last slide) so you can find them in a hurry in response to the question.

Ad Libbing a Dream

Martin Luther King's "I Have a Dream" speech is one of the most famous speeches in American history. Most people remember it for its passion and logic. What many don't know is its most famous passages were not scripted.

During the March on Washington, August 28, 1963, there were a number of speakers scheduled. Each speaker was given a time allotment, with Dr. King scheduled to speak last. His written speech timed out at just over four minutes.

As he spoke, he was encouraged by a woman in the audience, who kept yelling, "Tell them about the Dream, Martin." He physically put aside his written notes and began to speak from the heart. "I have a dream today," he began, "a dream that one day this nation will rise up and live out the true meaning of its creed: 'We hold these truths to be self-evident: that all men are created equal…'"

The rest is a 16-minute vision of the future that changed the world forever. He then concluded with his prepared close.

Understanding your audience and going "off message" to reach them can have powerful results. Don't be afraid to stray from your script as long as you know where it's going and how you want to finish your message to your audience.

Reading to Your Audience

Anyone with children will remember the first time they've been told, "Don't read that, Mommy (or Daddy), let me." That usually happens about age seven or so. Why then, would you want to read to audiences a lot older than that?

When they are read to, an audience questions your ability to be spontaneous, to really know your material, and even to question whether you wrote the presentation or not.

There are times you would want to read to an audience: when you're quoting a specific passage or set of numbers or when you want to put emphasis on something from another source of information. Here, though, are some suggestions.

- Let the audience know what you're quoting and why

- Keep the quote to a paragraph or two, then look up at your audience to cue them that the next words are your own

- Practice reading the passage out loud and mark it up for emphasis so that you avoid the sing-song quality that shows up in your voice when you read aloud

Borrow from the Best

Have you ever heard a speech or seen a scene in a movie that sums up what you want to say better than you could? Don't be afraid to use that to your advantage.

Quoting from popular culture is a great way to engage your audience, particularly younger audiences. First of all, they can often relate to a movie quote far better than to the words of some dead philosopher, and secondly they have the mental image of the movie scene in their head, which can add to the impact of your words.

For those of us who can't remember these things verbatim, here's a web source: www.americanrhetoric.com. It has audio, video, and text scripts of some of the most famous inspirational speeches from movies such as *Braveheart, Brian's Song, Henry V*, and many others.

Don't try to pass the words off as your own. Quote the source and have fun with it. As the director Peter Bogdanovich once said when accused of copying Orson Welles in one of his movies: "It's not plagiarism, it's an homage."

The Magic of Stories

One way to cut down on the amount of data you need to support your presentation to an internal audience might be to just tell a good story.

According to Peg C. Neuhauser's book, *Corporate Legends and Lore: The Power of Storytelling as a Management Tool*, telling stories is a great way to engage your audience and make abstract or complex concepts understandable.

People can relate more to stories than statistics, she says, and they create an emotional component and context that raw numbers don't create on their own. She identifies different types of stories to accomplish different ends, including Hero Stories, Survivor Stories, Letting Off Steam Stories, and Kick in the Pants Stories.

How well do you and your team tell your stories?

Anticipate Objections

"He who has truth at his heart need never fear the want of persuasion on his tongue."
- John Ruskin, British poet (1819-1900)

With all due respect to John Ruskin, it's not as easy to convince an audience as just having the "truth at your heart." To be truly persuasive, you must look at your call to action from the audience's perspective. Here are a couple of techniques for planning your presentation for greatest acceptance:

- Brainstorm and write down possible audience objections, then write specific responses that will overcome those objections.

- Your strongest argument will contain benefits to the audience before benefits to you or your organization. Asking someone to change the way they work because it will be better for the company is less likely to get real buy-in than if it will benefit them directly.

- Offer evidence to support any claims. If something is going to reduce time to market, explain precisely how. This is particularly true if you are asking people to change the way they do something that may add to their workload.

- The more the change affects them personally, the more personal the benefits should be.

Beautiful Words

What words make you feel warm and happy? Sure, it's different for all of us, but there are some words with universal appeal (at least in English). The British Council, which oversees education in the English Language, conducts an annual study of the "Most Beautiful Words In the English Language." 35,000 people participated in the study. The top ten words were:

1. Mother
2. Passion
3. Smile
4. Love
5. Eternity
6. Fantastic
7. Destiny
8. Freedom
9. Liberty
10. Tranquility

How many of these words can you weave into your next presentation to boost the positive energy? For the full list go to this website: 70 Most Beautiful Words Survey (http://www.britishcouncil.org/home-70-beautiful-words.htm)

"Great Moments in Communication"

345 BC LACKING POWERPOINT ACCLAIMED ORATOR DEMOSTHENES GIVES PRESENTATION TO THE ATHENIAN ASSEMBLY, PROVIDING VISUAL AIDS BY MAKING SHADOW PUPPETS IN THE LIGHT OF AN OIL LAMP

Powerpoint™

Do You Hate PowerPoint?

If you're one of the people who claim to hate PowerPoint, you're not alone. A recent Google search of the words "I hate PowerPoint" returned an astonishing 1,090,000 hits.

We at Communispond do not hate PowerPoint, but we definitely empathize with those of you who have been the victims of poor presentations. It's obvious that the golden rule of "do unto others" applies.

Don't present anything to an audience you wouldn't sit through yourself. Fair enough?

How Much PowerPoint?

According to an expert in high-level presentations, the higher level you're presenting to, the fewer PowerPoint slides you really need.

Rick Gilbert, author of *Speaking to the Big Dogs: A Boardroom Survival Kit*, says that when you reach the rarefied air of the boardroom, less is definitely more. "Be prepared for a dialogue, not a monologue," he says. "I recommend only three slides for every ten minutes."

Additionally, he says there is one thing to remember to help control nerves: "Bear in mind that the big dogs are on your side." His theory is that if they weren't positively disposed to your idea, you'd never have gotten to the boardroom, so relax and tell them what you want to tell them with no hedging or extraneous detail.

This Might Seem Minor...

A recent study of college students revealed a pet peeve they have with their professors that is important for all of us: Don't stand in front of the projector.

Presenters frequently move without being conscious of where they are in relation to the projector. As a result, they block the projected image with their bodies. Unless they wear white shirts and have very broad chests, this makes viewing the image difficult for the audience.

The study revealed that this seemingly minor presentation issue grates on an audience's nerves more than you might think.

Try moving forward from the side of the screen, rather than moving in front of it. When you move forward, take a quick look down to ensure you're not seeing patches of light on your clothing. If you are, your audience is missing at least part of the show.

Take care of the little details and your presentation will have a chance to shine.

What Sign Painters Know

How do you determine the right font size for a presentation? Sign painters have always judged the size of the print needed by the distance of the reader. They work from the rule that one inch is readable at 10 feet, two inches at 20, and so on. One inch on your screen is a 72-point font, but there's a caveat:

This is a great rule for flip charts, banners, and charts. It doesn't apply as directly for PowerPoint.

Take a look at your presentation *as you'll see it projected, not as it appears on your computer screen.* Unless you're presenting on your laptop, you don't need to use the largest fonts. The default sizes in PowerPoint (44 for titles, for example) work just fine.

Handouts vs. Presentations

Presenters are often faced with the challenge of how to create PowerPoint visuals that can be used later as handouts. The dilemma is usually this:

- Good presentation visuals are sparse, few in number, and don't use whole blocks of text where bullets will suffice

- Handouts need to be understood after the fact, studied and given to people who were not present

We offer two solutions, both of which require some work but will get you better results:

- Do the long "handout" version of the presentation first and save it as a separate file. Then, go through and clean it up, reducing the number of slides, simplifying graphics and editing text to the necessary minimum. Use the short version to present, and the more detailed version as a handout.

- Do a single, simple version, but add more details and examples in the "notes" section of the PowerPoint file. If they want additional information, they can simply print out the presentation with your notes.

Don't let the desire for easy handouts get in the way of your main presentation.

The Reverse Six

Do you have crowded technical visuals, but company policy or regulations won't allow you to simplify them? Well, work with what you have.

Web designers have a technique for making crowded web pages more clear. It's called the "Reverse Six." When you absolutely, positively can't make your PowerPoint slides any simpler, this might help.

The Reverse Six refers to how a reader looks at a web page. They start in the upper left, then look right and down and then up the left side and end up in the middle of the page. If you could draw the line, it would look like someone had drawn a six (6) across the page in reverse.

Try applying this as you clear complicated visuals to guide your audience. It's not as ideal as starting with simple, clear visuals, but it helps you make the best of what you have.

Some PowerPoint Text Tips

Here are some quick tips for using text on PowerPoint slides:

- Make text more legible by using a font size with a larger "X-height." Many fonts appear larger than others, even though they may have the same number size attached to them. You can tell those that appear largest by the height of the "x." For example, Ariel and Verdana fonts have larger X heights than Garamond.

- Remember the "4X4 rule" - Four lines per slide, four words per bullet.

- Whenever possible, use "sans-serif" fonts. They're easier to read from a distance. Serif is a fancy word for the little feet on letters in fonts like Times or Book Antiqua. Take a look at Arial, then look at Times. You'll see the difference.

Full Sentences vs. Key Words

One of the biggest areas of disagreement in the design of PowerPoint visuals is whether to use full sentences or simply key words. The answer lies in what you're intending to accomplish.

There are two options. You may want a document your audience can refer to and read at their leisure. Or you may want to create a visual cue that will help the presenter stay on track and be easy for the audience to remember. If you need to refer to it in depth, you'll want more detail. If it's simply visual support for your presentation, make it easy on yourself and use bullet points.

The more text on the slide, the less likely it will be for your audience to recall specific details. It will also serve as a distraction, since the audience will be reading while you're speaking.

Here's one place that full sentences do work well—in the title of the slide. If you title a slide something like "Our product will save you money," the audience will know what you're trying to accomplish, and your short bullet points will be better remembered.

F1 Stuff

Ever give a PowerPoint presentation and think, "Boy, it would be cool if

I could go back to that one slide without skipping through all the others"? You can do that and more, but it's hard to remember all the tricks. Need a quick memory refresher? Just hit the F1 key.

When you're in slide show mode, press the F1 key in the top left corner. A menu of very cool tricks will appear including:

- Hit the number of the slide you want and then press the enter key. You'll go to that slide without showing all the others.

- Hit the letter "B" to black out the screen.

- Hit the letter "W" to make the screen go white. This is kind of cool, but only useful if you're presenting against a whiteboard and want to show something on it.

Try it and see what presentation techniques are available. You'll look like you knew it all along.

Projecting the Right Image

One of the most common complaints about using a projector to show a PowerPoint presentation is that the picture is "cut off"—you can't see everything on the screen that is on your original visuals.

The most common reason for this is that the presentation was designed on a desktop computer in high resolution but the laptop you're working from doesn't have the same high-quality picture.

- From your computer's Start Menu, select "Control Panel"

- Click "Display"

- Click the tab marked "Settings"

There you'll find all the controls that send the picture from your laptop to the projector. Usually the problem can be solved by sliding the "Screen Resolution" indicator as far to the right as it will go.

When all else fails, connect the projector and reboot your computer. Although it takes a bit longer, odds are that the problem will self-correct.

Troubleshooting Projector Problems

Anyone who has had to present using PowerPoint and a projector has faced the moment when...nothing happens. Everything is set up but there's no picture, or the projector isn't getting a signal. You don't need to be a technical wizard or an engineer to easily troubleshoot the most common problems with this equipment. Just remember the mnemonic PCAP:

P Power: Do both your computer and your projector have electricity? Follow the power cords all the way from where they plug into the equipment to where they meet the wall. Make sure the power strip is turned on. (You'd be surprised how often that's the culprit!)

C Connections: Are the cables properly and tightly connected from the computer's port to the projector? Some projectors allow for more than one input: you may be in the wrong port.

A Application: Is your software working? Have you used the "function" key correctly? Have you been in PowerPoint and pushed the "B" button so the screen is blacked out?

P Projector: Is there a menu setting on the projector that isn't correct? If you have a remote control for the projector, check that it's functional.

When all else fails: Double check your connections, then reboot the computer with the projector powered on. Sometimes that's all it takes to get the pieces talking to each other correctly.

News Flash about Flash Drives

One of the coolest technology tools for presenters are the little "flash" or "jump" drives, which are small thumb-sized storage devices that plug into a computer's USB port. Presenters can store an entire PowerPoint presentation on them without worrying about CD-ROMs or armfuls of overhead transparencies.

Here are some tips for using your drives to best advantage:

- If at all possible, move presentations from the flash drive to the desktop of the computer you're presenting from. This is especially important if you have animation or a lot of special effects.

- Scan the presentation on your drive for viruses each time you add a new file or copy a file from someone else's computer. Portability can also be a security risk.

- While it's easy to simply add or remove a drive, it's best to use the "remove hardware" icon in the task bar so that your computer doesn't suffer stress from trying to read a disk that is no longer there. If you're using a Mac, just eject the drive with command+E before removing it.

Constructive Feedback on Building Visuals

Is it okay to use "builds" on PowerPoint visuals so as not to show everything all at once?

As with so much in life, there are no absolute answers, but here are some guidelines:

- Use them sparingly. Studies show participants don't like being kept in suspense.

- Don't overdo cute effects like flying, sound effects or spinning words. In fact, avoid them altogether in business presentations.

- Don't build the visual if you've already given the audience the complete slide in a handout. The surprise (and probably the reason for the build in the first place) is gone—why bother?

- Builds don't give you an excuse to put more than four bullets to a slide.

Drop the Mouse and No One Gets Hurt

More presenters are using remote or wireless mice to operate their PowerPoint presentations and the accompanying technology—but put the mouse down when you're done. Holding onto the mouse while presenting may:

- Create a distraction for you and your audience.

- Rob you of the ability to gesture freely and dynamically.

- Take you out of "sight" of the receiver, meaning the mouse doesn't do what you want it to. This can cause fumbling and reduce your credibility.

Find a convenient place like the lectern or a table to put the mouse down once you've advanced a slide so you know where it is and it won't distract from your power as a presenter.

Pointers for Pointers

For some reason, one of the most common questions we get is "What about the use of laser pointers to demonstrate on the screen?" Generally speaking, laser pointers serve as a toy for the presenter and an annoyance (at best) for the audience.

What are some alternatives? Try using the tools available in PowerPoint. When in "Slide Show" mode, click on "F1." You'll discover some neat tricks to augment your presentation such as:

- CTRL P = the marking pen appears. This allows you to highlight, circle, and annotate the image on the screen.

- CTRL A = an arrow appears. This is much better than a laser pointer since it remains steady, and can be con trolled easily by a mouse.

- Number followed by "Enter" takes you to that number slide...very useful for Q and A sessions when you want to reinforce your key points.

Keeping Updates Current

Do you give frequent updates, but don't want to update your PowerPoint visuals constantly? You can save time and money by embedding your graphs, charts, and tables as objects rather than as pictures.

If you use the tool bar to embed something as an object, then any changes to that object, such as addition of monthly numbers to a spreadsheet, automatically update the PowerPoint slide. If you present project or financial updates, this can help save you time and effort.

Just remember that the file you are showing must be on the same computer as the one you're presenting from, or it could be embarrassing come showtime!

The Power of Saving PowerPoint "Shows"

Have you ever been at a presentation where one presenter after the other has to boot their computer, open PowerPoint and go through their files, finally hit "view slide show" to get to their slides? Don't you wish there were an easier way to just get to it?

There is. Save your file as a .pps file, rather than a .ppt file. This option comes up when you hit "Save As..."

The .pps format saves your presentation as a full-screen

presentation. If it's on the desktop of your computer, and you click on the icon, it opens up in full screen glory, without having to put your audience through the whole process time and again.

Remember, you only want to do this with a fully finished presentation because you can't change the slides in this format.

An additional advantage is it makes the files much smaller and easier to email.

Converting PowerPoint to Pictures

Have you ever created a PowerPoint slide for a presentation—say a chart or graph—then wanted to use it in a handout package or include it in another document? It's easy to do: save it as a picture, instead of a PowerPoint presentation. Here's how it works:

- Find the slide you want to save in normal view

- Click File

- Click Save As Type

- Slide the dropdown arrow until you find "JPEG file interchange format"

- It will then ask you whether you want to save the entire presentation or just that file

- Once it's saved as a JPEG, you can cut and paste it into any document just as you would a piece of clip art Just be aware you can't change the JPEG file, you can only do that in PowerPoint.

PowerPoint Plus—Do You Need It?

If you've ever felt that most PowerPoint presentations look the same, you're not alone. An article in the *Chicago Tribune* (August 20, 2003) says there are over 40 companies creating software to augment the PowerPoint we're so familiar with in business.

Many, like Xcelsius, are designed to help turn data tables like spreadsheets and financial statements into more dynamic visuals. Others, like VoxProxy, use animation and moving clip-art to liven up children's Sunday school lessons.

These packages are usually designed because PowerPoint has become boring, and it's harder and harder for presentations to stand out. Are they necessary?

Like any other tool in your business "tool belt," PowerPoint or this extra software is only worthwhile if it helps you achieve your goals. What are you trying to accomplish? Our bet is that you'll find the power in your presentation lies in the message and the presenter, rather than the visuals that accompany your message. Use only the visuals you need to support—not overwhelm—your message or call to action.

More time spent in audience analysis and message preparation will serve you better than more color and flying letters. If you do need the visual support, choose carefully and make sure the style matches your audience's expectations and needs. A high-school class may respond well to chartreuse pie charts, the CFO might not. You know best.

"Great Moments in Communication"

982. ERIK THE RED, IN ATTEMPTING TO ATTRACT SETTLERS TO A NEW ARCTIC NEIGHBORHOOD, NAMES IT GREENLAND

PERSUASION

Words of Wisdom

"Truth persuades by teaching, but does not teach by persuading."
- Quintus Septimius Tertullianus,
Adversus Valentinianos Carthaginian church father (160 AD-230 AD)

What Brother Quintus was trying to say (and in Latin, no less) was that it is very difficult to persuade someone of truth through force of argument. The most effective way is to teach the audience something new, connect it to their world, and lead them where you want them to go.

Nine Principles of Persuasion

There are nine principles of modern persuasion:

- Every point of view is reasonable to the person who holds it

- Persuasion does *not* result from argument

- Persuasion begins long before you utter a single word

- Persuasion takes place in the mind of the persuaded, not the persuader

- The more channels you use to make your point, the greater the chance of persuading someone

- Visuals can never do the job alone

- Successful persuasion begins with trust

- Your message must be memorable, active or meaningful

- Persuasion never occurs if the message is unclear

How many of these principles do you follow when you attempt to persuade? Where do you need to brush up your skills?

Something to Think About

"Roughly speaking, any man with energy and enthusiasm ought to be able to bring at least a dozen others round to his opinion in the course of a year no matter how absurd that opinion might be."
-Aleister Crowley, British Occultist (1929)

While Crowley was one of the more controversial figures of the early 20th century, his point is an excellent one: a speaker's energy and enthusiasm captivate an audience and lay the groundwork for persuasion.

Energy and enthusiasm are intangible qualities that the audience sees and hears, including:

- Smiling

- Speaking at a strong volume

- Direct eye contact

- Use of positive, uplifting language

Just think what you can do with your opinions that aren't so absurd...

Napoleon's Motivators

"There are two levers for moving men—interest and fear."

Napoleon Bonaparte knew a thing or two about moving people to action, and his point was a good one. Whether the results are positive (an opportunity) or negative (fear of what will happen if you don't take action), people will respond better if they understand what the impact is on them.

It should be noted that Communispond does not advocate the use of grapeshot in making persuasive presentations.

Who Sits Where?

What is the correct way to seat yourself when making a sales presentation? When presenting while seated, the factors you need to consider are:

- Where is the decision maker sitting? Do you have a clear view of his or her face?

- As a rule, either end of the table provides more people a better view than somewhere in the middle.

- Why are you sitting? With more than three people, it will be difficult to make sure everyone can hear you.

Often, we sit during presentations because we are using handouts as opposed to "presenting." Don't be afraid to find an excuse to stand up. Go to a flip chart or white board. Sitting keeps a presentation informal and invites interruption and discussion.

Standing will add energy and excitement to your presentation and raise your stature in the eyes of your audience.

Aristotle's Wisdom

The ancient Greek philosopher Aristotle identified the three areas necessary to create powerful persuasive presentations. How do your presentations stack up?

- The appeal to reason

- The appeal to emotion

- The character and credibility of the speaker

A presentation lacking in any of these will be less powerful. A presentation where all of these are present is unbeatable.

When you create a presentation, do you build in elements that will boost the power of all three components? What's missing could make the difference between success and frustration.

Find the Bell Cow and Lead the Herd

Back in the old days, farmers used to put a bell around the neck of one cow in a herd. Among other reasons, it was to find the herd when they'd wandered away. What does that have to do with business presentations?

Well, the "bell cow" was the perceived leader of the herd, and the other cattle would follow her. Where you found the bell cow, you'd find the rest of the group. Every audience has at least one bell cow, and it may not be who you'd expect it to be.

Every group has individuals who represent the rest of the group. Sometimes that person is the oldest or most experienced, sometimes it's the person with the biggest title, or sometimes it's just an individual that has earned the respect and trust of the group at large.

To identify the bell cow in your audience, ask people who know the group who the opinion leaders are. They also tend to make themselves known pretty quickly, both by speaking out and by the references the rest of your audience makes to them. Winning them over will help guide the rest of your audience to where you want them to go.

Stoic Wisdom

The Stoic philosophers believed that it was a person's duty to accept things the way they are and not complain too much. One of their greatest writers was Epictetus (55-135 A.D.). He left us the following sage advice:

> *"All men's actions proceed from one source; that as they assent from a persuasion that a thing is so, and dissent from a persuasion that it is not, and suspend their judgment from a persuasion that it is uncertain, so likewise they seek a thing from a persuasion **that it is for their advantage**." (emphasis added)*

This doesn't mean that you can't change things, just that it's hard. If your audience sees their advantage in the position you're trying to persuade them to, you'll have a much easier time of it as a presenter.

He was also proof that accepting things are hard doesn't mean they can't change at all. Epictetus started life as a slave and ended up a respected and wealthy free man.

That turned out to the advantage of all of us.

"Social Proof"

When you're trying to persuade people to change problem-causing behavior, does it help to explain the magnitude of the problem? Not always, according to a team led by social scientist Robert Cialdini, who has made a career of studying influence.

Explaining the magnitude of the problem can undermine your persuasive message when you inadvertently supply negative "social proof." Cialdini's team ran a test at Petrified Forest National Park, which has been plagued by tourists carrying off pieces of petrified wood for souvenirs. The team created two signs: an injunctive one and a descriptive one. The injunctive one said, "Please don't remove the petrified wood from the park, in order to preserve the natural state of the Petrified Forest." The descriptive one said, "Many past visitors have removed the petrified wood from the park, changing the natural state of the Petrified Forest."

They found that in a control area with no signs, 2.92% of wood pieces were stolen. In the area with the descriptive sign, 7.92% were stolen. In the area with the injunctive sign, only 1.67% were stolen. It would seem that a message that gives an audience the "support" of other miscreants may be less effective in changing their behavior than a purely injunctive one and may even encourage the bad behavior!

For more information, see
http://www.insideinfluence.com/year06/05/torpedo.htm

Powerful Persuasion

Have you ever stopped to consider what it means to persuade someone?

In Communispond's book, *The Full Force of Your Ideas—Mastering the Science of Persuasion*, we look at the dictionary definition and take it even further.

According to the Random House Dictionary of the English Language, the word "persuade" means:

1. To prevail on (a person) to do something, as by advising or urging

2. To induce to believe by appealing to reason or understanding; convince

It's important to understand the difference between the two definitions. If you adhere to the second one, you'd think that the more "correct and logical" your argument, the more persuasive you'll be.

In business, we want to be logical and have our facts straight; yet it's important to realize that the first definition implies there are other forces—emotional factors—at work in persuasion.

Do your presentations contain both the facts and the emotional components that will truly sway an audience?

Persuasion Technology

Ordinarily, we think of presentation technology as PowerPoint and a projector. In fact, technology is anything we use other than our own bodies and minds to achieve a goal. The Wikipedia (a cool resource; check it out at www.wikipedia.org) gives examples of technologies that can be used for persuasive purposes:

• Books and pamphlets

• Impressive clothing (Louis XIV owned the lace factories that produced clothing useless for any purpose except emulating the King, thereby impressing others)

• Conventional mass media, such as print media, cinema, radio and television

- Presentation software and hardware, such as Microsoft PowerPoint, used with a data projector

- Subliminal advertising

- Computer simulation and modeling of electors and customers
- Computer and video games with deliberate presuppositions behind their scenarios

- Targeted mailing lists and email lists

What persuasive technology tools are you using to make your case?

"Great Moments in Communication"

1194, CHARTRES CATHEDRAL BURNS DOWN. THE BISHOP WRITES A LETTER TO ALL THE EUROPEAN RULERS PROMISING TO NAME A STAINED GLASS WINDOW FOR ANYONE WHO WILL MAKE A CONTRIBUTION TO REBUILDING IT, THUS INVENTING THE FUND-RAISING DIRECT MAIL LETTER.

EVERYDAY COMMUNICATION

How We Communicate

Do you know how we actually communicate? According to a study at the University of San Diego, adult Americans spend:

- 15% of the time *speaking*

- 17% of the time *reading*

- 15% of the time *writing*

- 21% of the time *mass listening* (radio, television, etc.)

- 32% of the time in *face-to-face listening*

Amazingly, in school most of us were taught to concentrate on reading and writing, which is where we spend only 32% of our time in the adult world!

Why Oral Communication Skills Matter

According to a 2004 study by the National Association of Colleges and Employers, the skills most desired in management-level employees are:

- Oral communication skills

- Interpersonal skills

- Analytical skills

- Teamwork skills

- Flexibility

- Computer skills

- Proficiency in a field of study

- Written communication skills

- Leadership skills

- Work experience

Notice that oral communication skills are more valued than actual subject matter expertise. Building these skills is a vital part of every professional's development.

A Snide Quote with a Point

"It usually takes three weeks to put together a good impromptu speech."

The American writer Mark Twain said this in jest, but he does raise an interesting point. A speech might be impromptu, but it doesn't mean there's no planning involved.

Use this format to quickly pull your thoughts together for a "good impromptu speech":

- Introduce the topic

- State your call to action or point of view

- Offer evidence

- Restate your call to action or point of view, and sit down before you start to ramble

It's Not Always What You Say. . .

"I understand a fury in your words, but not the words."
- Othello. Act IV. Scene 2.

In Shakespeare's *Othello*, Desdemona is accused of being unfaithful, even though she's innocent. She has no idea what she's being accused of, but knows it can't be good, and sure enough, it doesn't end well for anyone.

How we say the things we say is often as important as the words themselves. People pick up nonverbal and vocal cues that convey powerful messages. Are they consistent with what you're trying to say?

Start with Agreement

"If men would consider not so much wherein they differ, as wherein they agree, there would be far less of unchari-tableness and angry feeling."
- Joseph Addison, English essayist, poet, & politician (1672 - 1719)

Not only is this great advice on how to get along, it helps us communicate effectively in everyday situations.

By starting in agreement ("There is no argument; we have to increase our sales...") you create an environment in which mutual goals are established. This will earn you a more respectful hearing than if you start with "You're wrong, and here's why..."

Let's face it, there's enough "uncharitableness" in business as it is.

When You Have to Say "No"

Many people don't like saying "no" to others, even when someone asks them to do something that makes them uncomfortable or violates their standards. Here are some ways of saying "no" without damaging a relationship or ending a negotiation:

- Always explain why you can't agree to the request

- If possible, frame it to the other person's benefit or stated goal (e.g., "You might get it for a lower price elsewhere, but it could lead to expensive repairs down the road, which you said is part of the problem now...")

- Ask an easily answered question such as, "Would you like to discuss a solution I think *might* work better?"

An initial "no" doesn't mean the end of the conversation. It's an opportunity to educate the person making the request, show them options they may not have considered, and prove you're interested in helping them achieve their goals while maintaining your integrity.

.05 Seconds That Matter

Scientists have proved that even people who can effectively mask their emotions often use give-away cues like flinching, blinking, or smiling, but these cues can last as briefly as 1/20 second.

People, however, are really good at picking up these nonverbal cues—if they know to watch for them. Here are a couple of things to keep in mind:

- The more familiar you are with someone, the easier it is to read these signals

- These signals are universal: a flinch is a flinch is a flinch, seemingly anywhere in the world

- You have to be watching for them, which means making eye contact when you deliver a piece of information or ask a question

- The more different ways you ask a question, the more consistent the response

- You want to match these reactions to what they're saying, which means listening closely

Seven Rules of the Phone Message

The amount of business done over the phone each year is increasing. Not surprisingly, so are complaints that messages don't get returned properly. Part of the reason may be that we—or our assistants, or our kids, depending on where we work—have forgotten how to take a phone message. Here are the seven steps to a successful phone message:

1. Caller's name (and get the spelling)

2. Caller's company or affiliation

3. Time and date of the call

4. Who they're calling for (do they ask for you by name, ask for a rep, have no idea who they're looking for...)

5. Caller's number (with extension)

6. Purpose for the call (returning your call, looking for information...)

7. Any action items or instructions

You'll find you get better responses if you use this structure when you leave your own messages as well.

Your Absence Doesn't Make Their Hearts Grow Fonder

Think there's no difference between negotiating on the phone, web or other virtual media and negotiating face-to-face? A recent scientific study says otherwise.

A meta-analysis of research done at DePaul University on negotiating shows a noticeable rise in the number of "hostile acts" committed during telephone negotiations, versus negotiations where the two parties can fully interact.

Hostile acts are behaviors that reflect negatively on the individual committing them:

- Lying

- Threatening

- Using aggressive language

- Name calling

Negotiators that worked face-to-face with the other party showed less hostility and actually reported higher profits (sales, concessions from the other party) than those on the phone or the web.

Be aware of how you can sound to others when you can't look them in the eye.

Disagree with Your Boss, and Live to Tell About It

Mend your speech a little,
Lest it may mar your fortunes.
King Lear. Act I, Scene 1

Even in the 17th century, it was apparent that what you say has consequences. Of course, back in those days saying the wrong thing, especially to a king like Lear, could have consequences far more dire than anything we face at work. (If not, contact your HR department immediately.)

How can you make sure that you say what you have to say without "marring your fortunes"? In a recent *New York Times* article, Communispond founder Kevin Daley talked about how to constructively disagree with your boss. Among his tips were:

- Start by asking the boss what he or she wants to achieve in the meeting. That will help you focus your points on helping them achieve their end goals.

- Put yourself in the boss's place. For maximum buy-in, it's vital the boss see this as helping them achieve their aims—not prove the boss wrong.

- Don't use the word "but." It negates everything that's come before it. What you want to do is add to the boss's idea (use "and" instead of "but") or "suggest" other options that may make the goals easier to reach.

Five Steps to Networking

You need a personal network. If you didn't need to rely on people outside your family and work team, you wouldn't be reading this book. Sales professionals, who live and die by the effectiveness of their networks, say there are five steps to adding a person to one:

1. *Awareness.* They know who you are and what you do.

2. *Interest.* They express interest and ask for general information about you and your services.

3. *Trust.* They start to share information and ask for advice or information about specific issues or areas of interest.

4. *Desire.* There is a specific request for help.

5. *Close.* You do business with the person.

Understanding is More than Listening

If you ever wondered how important understanding is to business, think about this: according to a recent report, 60% of IT projects that fail do so because the client didn't effectively communicate.

According to Joseph Goguen, a professor at University of California San Diego, this is not because the IT people didn't listen well—the clients simply did not communicate their needs properly. What could the IT people have done better? Here are some ways you can help a client know what they don't know—and make the project more successful for everyone:

- If you don't hear questions you'd expect to hear, raise the subject yourself

- If there are potential problems that you have experienced and don't hear it from the client, ask if they've thought of those things

- Tell stories about clients so that "big picture" people can envision the results; they often don't get that vision from a spec sheet

The Power of the Echo... Echo... Echo....

Here's a reminder about a simple conversational tool for getting another person to give you more information about facts and feelings: Use an echo.

Echoing is simply repeating a specific word or phrase the other person has used to encourage them to elaborate.

For example, the other person says, "If I don't get this replaced by Thursday, it's my head."

You reply, "Your head?"

This encourages the person to tell you more about the consequences of failure in more accurate detail—after all, the odds of them actually losing their head over a business problem are not very good, but you will learn more about their specific situation (and the feelings surrounding it), and they will feel better understood.

Claiming Credit for an Eternal Truth

"I have often repented speaking, but never of holding my tongue."

Ever heard that quote? You're not alone. Books and websites that offer quotes attribute it to no fewer than seven people in four cultures and time periods, from Xenocrates or Simonides in Greece to Lao Tze and Samuel Johnson. Regardless of who actually said it first, when that many smart people say something, there's probably wisdom in it.

When do you speak and when do you hold your tongue? Here are some guidelines to when keeping silent might be the best plan:

- Are you adding new information or insight to the discussion, or simply rehashing what's already been said?

- Are you simply "piling on" someone whose idea is obviously going to be rejected? What good will that do?

- Is what you're about to say backed up by evidence or authoritative sources?

By asking yourself these questions before chiming in at a meeting or a presentation, you'll help ensure that what you have to say is of value to your audience. After all, any worth you have in the eyes of customers or employers is based on their perception of how you can help them achieve their goals. Knowing when to speak is just as important to that perception as shining when you do.

Tics Talk

A simple frown can cost you and your company more than you thought. Studies with consumer focus groups show that frowns, smiles, raised eyebrows, and other facial "tics" are a better indicator of their feelings than what they tell facilitators.

According to market researcher Dan Hill (in the book, *The Body of Truth*), a scientific principle called "facial coding" says that the small involuntary moves our faces make can display our real immediate reaction to presentations or messages. This happens unconsciously in microseconds. Once we have time to process the data we put on our best face and respond how we "think" we should.

In other words, that smile you're getting from a colleague may not be their true first reaction.

The theory surrounding this principle has been around for centuries, but new technology that can capture even slight reactions in digital pictures has enabled psychologists and other scientists to at long last prove what we've known all along. It's important to "read" non-verbal communication as well as to probe when you suspect there are mixed messages being sent.

Word Choices

You've always heard, "It's not what you said, it's how you said it." Sometimes, though, it is what you say that gets you into trouble. The words you use have an emotional impact on your listener.

Some words trigger negative emotional responses in people. For example, consider "problem" vs. "topic for discussion." In most listeners, the word "problem" inspires an immediate physical reaction: their defense mechanisms kick into gear. After all, there's a problem to be solved, and they need to be alert. If the topic at hand is perceived as a threat, there is a higher chance that the listener will become defensive or guarded in their response.

Other words that inspire similar reactions are:

- Consult vs. check with (consult sounds much more formal and ominous)

- Lie vs. mislead (lie is deliberate, mislead might be an unintended consequence)

- Consequences vs. results (consequences usually implies a negative outcome, usually a penalty of some kind, while results are emotion-neutral)

While all the words mentioned above are perfectly fine words and may be said in neutral tones, be aware of possible listener reaction when choosing your words, or you may make a difficult message even more difficult for you and those you're communicating with.

Getting Live People on the Phone

One of the most frustrating things about prospecting is getting voicemail and leaving message after message. How much better would it be to reach a living person? Here are a couple of tips for reaching someone other than a voicemail recording:

- *Call at strange hours.* If it seems that even during normal business hours you can't get a live person, odds are they're screening their voicemail. Try calling before 8:00 a.m. or after 6:00 p.m. If they're still at their desk, they're less likely to screen and more likely to pick it up.

- *Check the time stamp on their email.* If you've had email contact with these folks, check what time of day that email gets sent. Many people have consistent patterns of when they do tasks like answering email. Those are the times they're most likely to be "at home" and picking up.

- *Leave who you are until after what they need.* Even though it can be a frustrating exercise to leave a voice mail and never know if they're going to delete it before you can get their interest, they can be made more effective. Many experts suggest not giving your name or company name until the end of the message.

Too Much of a Good Thing

Can you have too much of a good thing? Abraham Lincoln certainly thought so. While he appreciated and excelled at the art of oration (public speaking being even more in demand in the 19th century than it is now) he also knew it had its pitfalls: "Extemporaneous speaking should be practised and cultivated. It is the lawyer's avenue to the public... And yet there is not a more fatal error to young lawyers than relying too much on speechmaking." (Law Lecture, 1851)

How do you practice and cultivate the skills and yet not rely too much on "speechmaking"? Try these tips:

- Don't speak until you can clearly state your point of view in a single sentence.

- Be able to offer specific evidence, rather than generalities or vague feelings.

- Know how to end effectively. Often simply restating your point of view ("So that's why I say...") will be better than just running out of words to say.

Don't forget the second half of the quote, though. Relying too much on speechmaking can make you seem starved for attention and increase the chances that you'll say something you regret.

Pick your opportunities and make them work to increase your value in the eyes of your colleagues and co-workers.

Speaking on the Spot

Do you tend to ramble when you ad-lib a speech? Remember the four-step "speak on the spot" format. It may sound stilted at first, but if you get used to using the lead-ins, you won't get off track:

1. "I have something to say about (the topic under discussion)."

2. "The way I see it (state your specific recommendation or point of view)."

3. "The reason I say that is (back up your statement briefly with supporting evidence)."

4. "So that's why I say (re-state your recommendation or point of view as a way of knowing when to wrap up and sit down)."

If you need to offer more detail, let your audience ask for it. It's better than drowning them in detail and getting yourself lost.

Five Messages that are Inappropriate for Email

- "We can't work together any more."
- "Great job!"
- "In response to your question…"
- "You need to improve."
- "Here's how to do it."

The reason these messages are inappropriate for email is that each one is a conversation opener. Email is a great way to exchange bits of information or to ask brief, closed questions. But whenever you say one of these things, you're beginning interpersonal engagement. For some of them, like firing somebody, you need to be in the person's presence. For others, pick up the phone.

Get in Touch With Your Inner Horse

No one today doubts the importance of body language in communication, but if you want a dramatic story to illustrate its importance, consider the case of Clever Hans.

Hans was a horse whose trainer taught him to do arithmetic and to answer questions about spelling, reading, and music. All the questions were posed to the horse in a form that allowed him to answer with numbers, which he provided by tapping his hoof on the ground the appropriate number of times. He was a sensation, and in 1907, psychologist Oskar Pfungst performed a series of tests to determine whether Hans could actually count.

Pfungst could find no evidence of fraud, but he determined that Hans was unable to answer questions when the questioner did not know the answer. Through careful observation, he discovered that Hans read changes in a questioner's posture and facial expression to determine when he had reached the correct number of hoofbeats.

Having explained Hans's abilities, Pfungst put his theory to the test with a series of laboratory tests in which he played the part of the horse. He found that 90% of the people who participated in his experiments gave him cues sufficient to allow him to answer the questions.

Use Holiday Messages Wisely

Near the end of the year, managers and business leaders like to send out holiday messages to their employees, customers, and investors. The messages can be warmly accepted or shrugged off. What separates the grand from the bland?

- *Make it personal.* General well wishes can sound hollow without personal examples or people's names. "Karen, Buffy, and I..." sounds more natural than "From all of us to all of you."

- *Make it sincere.* Try to use the words you'd use in conversation, not words that sound corporate and flat.

- *Make it more than once a year.* If you communicate often, then the holiday message is perceived as a holiday message, and not that once a year obligation. You'll also not be tempted to cram a year's worth of information into a message, making it warmer and more focused on the occasion.

"Great Moments in Communication"

1453 IN AN EFFORT TO REDUCE THE RUINOUS COST OF MAKING HANDOUTS FOR GUILD MEETINGS, JOHANNES GUTENBERG INVENTS MOVABLE TYPE AND THE PRINTING PRESS

MEETINGS AND ORGANIZATIONS

The High Cost of Wasted Time

Have you ever wondered what it costs to have a meeting?

Simply taking the hourly pay of each attendee and multiplying it by the amount of time they spend in the presentation is only the beginning. Take the example of a senior manager in a one-hour sales presentation that doesn't hit the mark:

- One hour of the manager's time *plus*

- One hour of productivity that could have been spent somewhere else *plus*

- At least an hour of venting and telling everyone how unproductive the meeting was *plus*

- Travel time to and from the meeting *plus*

- The costs of another meeting—possibly with a different presenter who can make it worth their while—*times*

- The number of people in the meeting

Now imagine the topic of your presentation is, "How we can save your company money."

Not achieving your aim can cost them—and you—more than just time. Good audience analysis pays off in more substantial ways than you'd think.

Meeting Experts

If you're someone who wants to make a mark in your company, here's an idea: become a meeting expert. Studies show that executives spend almost half their time in meetings (either in person or on the phone). Someone who can run a good meeting can actually boost productivity and be a valuable asset to the organization.

It's a misconception that the person running the meeting needs to be the boss or the person heading a project team. A good meeting facilitator needs to:

- Be able to set an agenda and keep people on track

- Understand the desired outcomes of the meeting and know the best techniques for reaching them—information meetings are different than problem-solving meetings

- Know how to solicit feedback from all participants and keep them engaged

- Know at least three ways to help teams brainstorm

One advantage to having you, as a third party, run work-team or departmental meetings is you can get more balanced feedback, and the "boss" becomes a little less intimidating and more of a true teammate.

Problem-Solving or Problem-Causing?

When running a problem-solving meeting, do you find your team re-hashing old solutions, getting off topic and losing focus? The problem may be how you present the problem. Present a problem statement and a description.

Problem Statement. Define the problem and the cause of the problem, or the object and defect.

Description:

- What is the problem?

- Where did it occur?

- When does it occur?

- What is the magnitude of the problem?

Once these details have been defined, your team can stay focused on the task at hand and you can check bad assumptions at the door.

Defining the Problem

When conducting a problem-solving meeting, how you define the decision you have to make goes a long way toward determining the quality of the solution.

Many times we put the solution we're looking for in the description. There's a big difference between these two statements:

- "We need to hire more people because there's a backlog in Accounts Receivable."

- "We have a backlog in Accounts Receivable. We think the problem may be head count."

One statement clearly constricts the possible solutions, while the other opens the door for true discussion, checking of assumptions and quality answers.

Are you clearly defining the problem or making assumptions?

You Don't Need to Meet to Read

One way people are reducing the number of ineffective meetings is to have strict criteria about when a meeting is appropriate. According to Kenneth Sole, author and OD consultant, one time a meeting is *not* appropriate is when you're simply presenting data.

"Why get people together if everything is written down in reports?" he asks. People can read the information for themselves. He recommends using that valuable meeting time only when there is strategy or action to be planned. That's when getting people together really adds value.

Making the most of people's time is both respectful and good business.

Presenting While Sitting...

As a business professional, you probably spend a great deal of time in meetings. Here are some guidelines that can increase your effectiveness no matter what you're trying to accomplish in a small group situation.

- Position yourself so you can make easy eye contact with all participants.

- Make sure you maintain eye contact with everyone, but save the really important points for your decision maker(s). Look them squarely in the eye when you talk dollars or deliverables.

- Sit up comfortably but don't slouch or have your back against the chair. Sit upright and forward on the seat.

- Drop that pen...it will only become a drumstick or a baton or some other distraction. If you're taking notes, write down what you heard then put the pen down.

Feedback Is a Gift

"Oh, to see ourselves as others see us."
- Robert Browning (1850)

A new technology company is going in front of Wall Street analysts in a week. The figures are right, the business plan is solid, everyone is in accord. What's the next step? Back to the boardroom with a coach to hone the presentations— because if you don't present yourself effectively, investors won't buy your vision of the future. Stakes don't come much higher.

This is not a hypothetical situation. Successful companies know how vital their public face is to their success. Whether from a professional expert or simply a peer using a checklist, having another person offer you feedback on your presentation before the fact is one of the strongest guarantors of presenting success.

Nothing you will ever do as a presenter will have the impact of receiving immediate feedback on your presentation. Among the things you can not know for yourself are

- Is your content clear to people hearing it for the first time?

- Do you look comfortable with the presenting technology you'll use?

- Are you making eye contact, gesturing effectively, and demonstrating the courage of your convictions?

Team Presentations

Team presentations offer unique challenges, but business presents more and more opportunities for them, especially in sales.

Here are some hints for making good team presentations:

- Have each team member introduce the following person. No need to do unnecessary hand-offs, and the audience is impressed by the teamwork.

- At the beginning of the presentation, introduce each team member and tell the audience what they'll speak on, for how long, and their relevance to the project or presentation. This helps the audience set expectations.

- Use a common template for presentation visuals and handouts. The presentation should look like one big unit, rather than cobbled-together pieces.

Keeping Friends in High Places

If you want to be seen as an asset to the senior people in the organization and make friends in "high places," use less PowerPoint.

It may seem counter-intuitive, but the higher you go in an organization, the less detail is usually required, and that's where most of us tend to overload our presentation. Senior executives as a rule want to know the "big picture," with enough detail to support your recommendation or analysis.

If details are needed, they are probably in more depth than a PowerPoint slide can easily convey and you're better off using handouts for reference.

Sometimes You're the Audience

"Speech belongs half to the speaker, half to the listener. The latter must prepare to receive it according to the motion it takes."
- Michel de Montaigne (1533-1592), French essayist

Let's take a look at presentations from the other side—when you're an audience member.

As Montaigne says, the listener must prepare to meet the speakers where they are and follow along. As an audience member, be prepared to put some work into listening, and if it's going somewhere you don't understand or can't follow, ask questions to help the speaker meet your needs.

Of course, as a speaker, you should make it as easy on your audience as possible and make sure the "motion" takes them in to consideration and doesn't leave them far behind.

Lessons from History

Good communication is essential in any organization—and may have won the battle of Gettysburg for the Union in the U.S. Civil War.

According to the Reserve Officers Association, a historical group that gives leadership seminars at the Gettysburg battlefield, a contributing factor in the Union victory was that the Northern Army was a cohesive unit with clear orders. The South, under General Robert E. Lee had many new officers with unclear chains of command.

According to retired U.S. Colonel John O'Shea, a spokesman for the group, the Union Colonel Joshua Chamberlain had unambiguous orders to defend the Union flank at all costs. All his subordinates knew the orders. When his troops ran out of ammunition, he ordered a bayonet charge. He knew what to do and when.

Lee, with unfamiliar commanders and a chaotic signal system, was unable to respond in a quick, coordinated fashion. The result changed history forever.

New Manager Blues

The first 90 days of a new manager's tenure often determines his or her ultimate success or failure in the role. Managers who seem to be in control, communicate effectively, and send the right signals of confidence and openness right away tend to be more successful in the long run than those who start off on the wrong foot with their direct reports.

Harvard Business School researcher Dr. Michael Watkins reports in his book, *The First 90 Days*, studies of hundreds of managers who were hired with high expectations, but ultimately were unsuccessful. Among his findings were:

- Managers who are uncomfortable with their new role often send non-verbal signals, what Watkins calls the "hunted look in their eye." This is particularly prevalent with high performers moving to their first management job.

- Managers who don't communicate well undermine their employees' faith in their abilities.

- Senior management and business owners tend to put new managers in place and don't monitor their first few weeks very carefully, thereby missing opportunities to catch and coach mistakes before they become a permanent part of the manager's reputation.

How well do you or your organization support new managers? Do you have the support and educational systems in place to help those first 90 days set the right mood?

Creating Corporate Culture

Merger and Acquisitions experts say that the hardest part of blending two or more companies together is to create a single unit out of all the parts—many of whom may have been competitors before the purchase. The key to successful blending? Communication.

Part of the communication challenge is the message to be communicated. This is usually easier than the second part: ensuring that the message gets communicated the same way to all portions of the company.

Is there a company-wide standard for delivering information and a methodology for checking its consistency?

Do managers at the line level know the message and how it's expected to be delivered? Messages that sound good when they leave the corporate office are often watered down and become one-line emails by the time they get to managers in the field.

Creating a corporate culture often begins with a commitment to consistency of message as well as consistency of delivery.

Look Confident, Be Confident

In the February, 2003 issue of *Inc.* magazine, a British psychologist claimed that we exude confidence because we act confidently, not the other way around.

Ros Taylor hosted a television show called "The Confidence Lab." This program took 12 shrinking violets through a number of exercises, from posture to salsa lessons. Within nine months, all had asked for and received promotions, landed prestigious new jobs, and—in two cases—launched companies.

"Psychologically, action precedes change," insists Taylor. "If you start doing things in a more confident fashion, it feeds back to your nervous system that you might actually be confident. All these people went through profound cognitive shifts about what they could do internally."

Kevin Daley, founder of Communispond, says that's something Communispond has taught since its inception. "We often are seduced by the belief that the attitude of confidence comes first and confident actions then follow. Not so. Confidence is created through successful experiences. That's what confidence is all about...doing a thing successfully often enough to know you will be successful the next time. The skills come first and a confident attitude comes in response to being skillful...not the other way around."

Flattery Revisited

A recent University of Washington study reveals something about job seekers that's relevant to anyone who works in an organization: it's better to flatter than to brag.

The study looked at job seekers and the recruiters who interviewed them. People who flattered the interviewer received higher ratings than those who expounded on their merits.

They received those ratings because interviewers believed they shared their beliefs and attitudes, indicating a potentially good fit at the company. This tells you something about getting along in an organization, but it also says something about communication. If you need to persuade someone, ingratiating yourself through appropriate levels of flattery (nothing obvious or obnoxious, of course) may help you more than your own impressive credentials.

Communication and Your Stock Price

Communication training can increase a company's stock price. That assertion may sound implausible, but please bear with us while we show you the relationship.

According to Sirota Survey Intelligence, which has been tracking this phenomenon for at least two years, company stock price correlates closely to employee morale. In 2005, for example, companies with high morale increased their stock prices 240% faster than other companies in the same industry.

What does that have to do with communication training? High-morale companies, according to Sirota, provide three main things to employees: 1) fair treatment, 2) a sense of achievement in their work and pride in their employer, and 3) good, productive relationships with fellow employees. Numbers (2) and (3) are directly correlated to effective communication training.

"Great Moments in Communication"

VIRTUAL MEETINGS

Three Technologies for Meeting Without Being There

There are essentially three types of virtual presentation tools available. Each has its pros and cons:

1. Teleconferences. These are easy to arrange, not terribly expensive, and can get a lot of information out to a large audience in a hurry. On the minus side, it's hard to keep people engaged, and not a viable method for sharing visual information.

2. Web Meetings. These meetings usually have audio via the telephone, but add visual components. These components include PowerPoint presentations controlled by the presenter or shared by the audience, and the ability to interact, using polling and other tools. They require a lot of bandwidth and can be interminably long.

3. Video Conferencing. This tool allows the audience and presenters to "put voices to faces." The downside is the high cost, and the technology usually limits the other parts of your presentation.

The trick to being effective is deciding what you want to accomplish with that audience. Although each device has its uses, choose the right tool for the job.

The Poor Man's Webinar

If you're dealing with an audience of varied technical sophistication and capability, you can have a pretty decent online meeting without having to use either a server or dedicated software.

Distribute your presentation to participants in advance as a PDF file and conduct the meeting by conference call. Almost every computer user in the world has a program capable of opening and displaying PDFs, and everybody in business has a telephone.

Be sure to tell the audience explicitly what "page" they should be on every time you move to a new slide, in order to keep them from wandering unsupervised through the PDF.

This kind of setup doesn't allow for polling or document sharing or many of the other things that make webinars so engaging, so you'll have to make up for that with tone of voice and compelling material. But you should be using those things no matter how advanced your technology is.

Rules for Web Meetings

Anyone who has run a web meeting or teleconference knows how hard it can be to maintain attention for any length of time. Here are some rules to help keep people engaged:

- Never schedule a meeting for longer than 45 minutes if you can help it; anything longer had better be life or death for participants

- Ask questions of participants periodically to keep them engaged

- Set ground rules at the beginning including "turn off your email"; the temptation to check email while online is overwhelming for many participants and will diminish their attention to the task at hand

Positive Pauses

Using visuals on conference calls or web-meetings may cause confusion with your audience. Frequently, presenters jump ahead, causing audience frustration and uncomfortable stoppages. Exercise patience and use delays and pauses to your advantage.

Whether reviewing a document during a conference call, or using a PowerPoint presentation in a web-meeting, the challenge is to keep people on the same page. One great way to do that is to plan your transitions effectively:

- Tell them you're finished with that visual and you're moving on

- Offer a transition statement to cover the visual changing on screen if appropriate

- Direct them to the next page or item ("now skip page six, but move to the middle of page seven"), then pause two seconds

- Check in to see that they have found the document, or are looking at the right visual on their screen (slow internet connections mean dense graphics don't appear instantly)

These tips not only reduce frustration but build in opportunities for interactivity and questions that will keep these presentations from becoming dull.

Check in Without Checking up

One of the challenges of communicating in a virtual world is the inability to look people in the eye and see if they're interested, engaged, or even present and accounted for. The challenge is to maintain contact verbally without seeming like you're checking up on people or being patronizing.

Here are some techniques for checking in with people without being too obvious about it.

- Throw out questions or opportunities for comment once in a while. Be aware that you'll probably get the same people responding over and over again.

- You have to involve the people who are out there but not answering, as well. Plan questions with someone specific in mind. Then, say their name and then the question ("Sue, what do you think about..."). If you do it this way, their name cues them that they're expected to respond and they won't be caught unprepared and embarrassed.

- Set expectations, like asking them to turn off their email. Getting an email from someone on the conference call or web meeting is usually a sign they're not listening too well.

- Tell people in advance you'll be asking for feedback, and what kind of specific things you're looking for. That way they can't claim to be surprised by your question.

Keeping a positive tone while setting firm expectations can help your teleconferences and web-meetings stay on track and keep people engaged without seeming too overbearing.

Presenting on Webcam

Giving a presentation via the web using a webcam is fun, and the technology is interesting, but it presents some interesting challenges. Here are some tips:

- *Don't make any sudden moves.* Depending on the bandwidth of your computer network (and that of your viewers) most webcams are still fairly low-resolution. This can lead to jerky pictures. Move slowly and deliberately.

- *Gesture away from the camera.* One of the big challenges about this technology is that it uses a "fish-eye" lens. It's a little like looking through an apartment door. At a distance the picture is fine; up close the image gets distorted. You can look like your arms are 17 feet long and reaching through the computer at the audience. It's a little disturbing.

- *Watch the lighting.* Make sure that you have your face in direct but not harsh light. If the light source is behind you, there is a chance all they'll see is a silhouette. You look less like a professional presenter and more like an anonymous source on the TV news.

Fishing for Responses

When you're on a teleconference, it's hard sometimes to know whether people are listening or answering their email. One way to check in with people is to go "fishing" for responses.

What this means is there are three types of questions you can ask:

- *Casting.* Pick an individual and throw them an easy question that lets them know they're expected to respond.

- *Trolling.* Ask the group as a whole for responses and take volunteers.

- *Net and Sort.* Throw the question out to the whole group, then intentionally pick someone you haven't heard from before. This helps shy individuals feel comfortable contributing and helps control those who always respond.

When you're fishing for responses, remember that recognition and affirmation are sometimes the best bait.

Eye Contact without the Eyes

Even good presenters struggle with teleconferences and web meetings. The lack of a visible audience leads them to do things they'd never do in a "real" presentation: read word-for-word from a page, look down and speak into their notes, ramble on or over-explain because they can't see impatience or understanding in the eyes of their audience.

Every person who's ever communicated with another person understands the importance of eye contact. You can communicate interest, challenge, credibility, and even love without saying a word. But what about when you can't see the person to whom you're speaking—or who's speaking to you? How do you make eye contact without the eyes?

- Look up and imagine your telephone or web audience sitting in a semi-circle around you. Then deliver your presentation by looking at those places.

- Use audience member's names, if appropriate. This will cue you to picture them and deliver the relevant information in a more connected manner.

- Check your presentation notes, then look away. Don't get trapped into speaking to the page. Your head will drop and your body language will change, making your volume and inflection much less interesting.

Volume, Even on the Phone

How many engaging, personable presenters become dull and lifeless on the telephone? Teleconferences become boring and people drift off into email, solitaire, or whatever is going on around them, and don't listen.

One reason is we tend to lower our volume when speaking on the phone. Sometimes this is out of respect for people in cubicles around us, but often it's just because we're self-conscious about speaking at a normal presentation volume when it's just us talking into a telephone.

Volume is important. It gives our voice inflection and color. If we don't speak at a normal speaking volume, we risk sounding monotonous to our audience.

Remember, without the visual component, your audience depends on your voice to hold their interest. Don't let them down.

Reviewers Hiding in the Weeds

If someone were to review your conference calls, would they give you a thumbs-up or a big thumbs-down? It could be happening as you read this.

In the October 2003 issue of *Fast Company* magazine, a writer for the magazine reviewed a conference call held by the Chairman of MCI. Michael Capellas was explaining to industry analysts and reporters what changes were being made to put the company's financial house back in order. In the words of the reviewer, "he had an opening statement, fielded more than a dozen questions, he had a closing statement—and he said absolutely nothing." If the call were a movie, it would be dead at the box office.

If the notion of someone doing a review of the conference calls you lead gives you chills, imagine what the participants on your call must experience. Here's what will get you raves instead of pans:

- Keep it short.

- Keep the audience's needs in mind. Find out what they want to get out of the meeting and make sure they get it.

- Keep the energy level high. Audiences can hear uncertainty in your voice almost as clearly as they can see it on your face.

One way to find out how people react to your conference calls is to have a supervisor, peer, or someone you trust listen in and give you feedback on the way you lead the call.

Better to get the review from a friendly honest source than to see it published in a magazine!

—